Enjoy Greater Results with *Less* *Effort*

Build a *Better You*

Bud Hendrickson

www.GreaterResultsLessEffort.com

Creative Team Publishing
Fort Worth, Texas

Disclaimers:
- o Due diligence has been exercised to obtain written permission for use of references or quotes where required. Additional quotes or references are subject to Fair Use Doctrine. Where additional references or quotes require source credit, upon written certification that such claim is accurate, credit for use will be noted on the book's website: www.GreaterResultsLessEffort.com.
- o Illustrations used in this book are true-life stories. The opinions and conclusions expressed are solely of the author and/or the individuals represented in the stories, and are limited to the facts, experiences, and circumstances involved. Certain names and related circumstances have been changed to protect confidentiality. All stories where names are mentioned are used with the permission of the parties involved. Any resemblance to past or current people, places, circumstances, or events is purely coincidental.

ISBN: 978-0-9855979-5-5

PUBLISHED BY CREATIVE TEAM PUBLISHING
www.CreativeTeamPublishing.com
Fort Worth, Texas
Printed in the United States of America

Permissions and Credits

o   Cover Photo: Taken from the deck of my home by my good friend, Dean Dew, the photograph of Mount Hood represents the new journey that my wife, Nancy, and I took leaving California. It is beautiful and brings much joy. It also represents a new life with Kristin, my new wife, whom I married following Nancy's death. The picture taken in the morning represents a new day and how it is a gift and we need to use it wisely. Also, a mountain can represent work to get to the top or summit. But once on top what a view you have! Life is much like that: it can be work but what a ride it can be!

o   All Scripture references are quoted from the New International Version (NIV) of the Holy Bible, unless otherwise noted. New International Version (NIV) Copyright © 1973, 1978, 1984, 2011 by Biblica

o   Logo concepts and Situation Figure were developed by Grant Hendrickson and Brett Hendrickson under direction from the author and are used with permission. The author has used the Situation Figure graphic representation over many years to communicate the value of diverse perspectives and skill sets in the work place.

Sourced References in Order of Appearance:

o http://www.ipwatchdog.com/2014/11/01/the-rise-and-fall-of-the-company-that-invented-digital-cameras/id=51953/

o http://www.sfgate.com/business/article/How-stars-so-rich-and-famous-can-go-broke-3226082.php

o Reference to quote by Jamie Notter, co-author with Maddie Grant of *When Millennials Take Over: Preparing for the Ridiculously Optimistic Future of Business* (IdeaPress Publishing, 2015), and blog located at http://jamienotter.com/2012/09/what-is-innovation/ is used with permission of Jamie Notter.

o Definition of 360 Feedback can be found at https://en.wikipedia.org/wiki/360-degree_feedback.

o https://en.wikipedia.org/wiki/Fostoria_Glass_Company

o The Personal Formula for Change is an adaptation by the author of various change diagrams used extensively in leadership and management training.

o Reference to *Leadership Is – How to Build Your Legacy* is used with permission of Glen Aubrey, Creative Team Publishing. www.CreativeTeamPublishing.com

Enjoy *Greater Results* with *Less Effort*

Build a *Better You*

Bud Hendrickson

Foreword

Mark Speckman
Assistant Head Coach, Running Backs Coach, University of California, Davis, and Public Speaker

It's a scary proposition to write a book about your life experiences. On one level, you are excited to see it completed and hope it will be a success. But on a deeper level, it is overcoming the fear that people will not think of you as presumptuous—a know-it-all. You hope your story resonates with people, and that your story can help people see their life with just a little different perspective.

In Bud Hendrickson's first book, *Enjoy Your Journey: Ten Bedrock Truths to Improve Everything About You*, he took that leap of faith. Bud's journey is uniquely his. Forged by values from his parents, and experiences he has gone through in growing up, he shares lessons learned as a young man and lessons he continues to learn. Continuing with experiences as a professional, a husband, and a father, he has quilted together stories and thoughts that we can all appreciate and learn from.

While this is a book about Bud's journey, it is a story we can all relate to. We are all on a unique journey and it is a gift to be reminded that others have traveled the same road. The themes he writes about are issues we all wrestle with, and the questions at the end of each chapter are helpful in reflecting your situation to **The Ten Bedrock Truths** Bud shares.

I know when I co-authored my book, *Figure It Out: How I Learned to Live in a Digital World Without Digits*, I really worried, "Does the world need another 'self-help' book?" What I have come to realize is that we all love a good story. We all are struggling with ways to better navigate our life's journey. Bud's book is a wonderful study of one man's journey, and it shines a light on all of our journeys.

It is scary to write a book about your life. Thankfully, people like Bud have the courage and conviction to share their lives. And we are all better for it.

www.speckmanspeaks.wordpress.com

You can obtain Mark Speckman's new edition of his book:

Figure It Out: How I Learned to Live Without Digits in a Digital World (Second Edition)

Available through Amazon.

Enjoy and Improve ... It's Your Choice

This book is a brand-new work based on Bud's first book, but updated and even more relevant to today and its future readers. Bud states, "Along my life's journey I have learned the importance of taking the responsibility and initiative to make better life choices, to build a better me, and build a better you. These choices have produced increased enjoyment for me along the way.

"The Statue of Liberty represents so much of what is good about our country. But liberty without responsibility leads to a society of chaos and stress. A Statue of Responsibility should be built as well, so that all could be reminded of the importance of how liberty and responsibility go hand in hand.

"I hope you value reading *Enjoy Greater Results with Less Effort*. The core idea is that no one makes choices for us. Life presents us with choices that we must make every day, to improve all aspects of our lives. My entire life I have chosen to take delight and pleasure in all that I did, from which, in turn, I have received benefit that I have enjoyed in every stage of life. I wouldn't necessarily say I would ever want to return to life's various stages, but I have enjoyed them, and look back with fondness on all my stages in life."

The results may be more than you could ever envision!

The Power of Relationships

This is a book about the power of relationships: with God, each other, and whomever we reach.

1. We all have the need to enjoy a relationship with God which is an enduring standard upon which to build any and all personal relationships with ourselves and other people.

2. We must love ourselves, following God's second great commandment, since we cannot give love to others if we don't already have it internally.

3. By building positive relationships within ourselves we can fully engage in creating and living in positive relationships with other people.

4. This power of transferable love relationships is available to all of us, anytime.

Dedication and Photographs

I would like to dedicate this work to my first life partner, Nancy, who was a part of my experiences and growth since our first date after the homecoming game in our sophomore year of high school. We celebrated our 16th birthdays together, got married, and had two boys to add excitement to our lives. When I add this up, our time together represents 70% of my life. Even though we had both good times and challenges along our life's journey, there was so much enjoyment and satisfaction along the way.

I also want to dedicate this book to my new wife, Kristin. We got married in 2019 after having dated for two years, following Nancy's passing in 2015.

God made men and women to be different from each other and together we are complete. I am a better man today because of the life and investment Nancy and I had in each other along the way, and I am sure Nancy would say the same if she was still alive. We complemented each other well and I am thankful for that.

Now Kristin is making me even better as we both strive to live for God, seek His will, and enjoy the journey!

Just as Nancy and I honored our parents and the legacy they demonstrated for us, I hope this book will document the legacy she and I want to leave for our boys and loved ones, as well as the new legacy Kristin and I are forming for our family and friends. Our journey was not and is not perfect, but we gladly take responsibility to make choices throughout both journeys, to increase the enjoyments we have had all along the way!

Nancy and Bud's Wedding, August 15, 1987, Custer, South Dakota
Photo by Carroll Photography, Custer, South Dakota

Bud and Kristin's Wedding, July 21, 2019, Washington.
Photo by Powers Photography Studios, Portland, Oregon

Table of Contents

Table of Contents

Table of Contents

Table of Contents

*****

Addendum:

*****

A History of Living and Learning

My first book, *Enjoy Your Journey * Ten Bedrock Truths to Improve Everything About You* was completed and published in August of 2016, one year after my high school sweetheart and wife of twenty-eight years passed away. I know what *Enjoy Your Journey* is in my mind, and some may think they are enjoying their journey now but don't realize there is even more to life available to them.

I contemplated how to respond effectively with very few words when someone would ask me what my book was about. I finally came across a good response, and wrote a blog on *Greater Results with Less Effort* in October of 2018. I felt that what I had learned in my life's journey was the importance of using the Bedrock Truths to focus on the highest priority issues, tapping into relationships and perspectives so that I would make the most informed choices I could on my journey.

By being more effective, it put me in a position to invest in others with time, energy, and money, to have positive impacts on others. That is why the new title, *Enjoy Better Results with Less Effort * Build a Better You* more accurately represents what the Bedrock Truths are all about.

We are creating our personal histories and legacies, all the time, literally every day. Life is all about learning and applying the multiple lessons we've taken in, teaching our immediate family the Bedrock Truths, understanding and accenting the strength of positive relationships through every phase of life.

In the book of Esther in the Bible, we read this phrase: "… for such a time as this." What it says is that you and I are "placed" here for a purpose. Will we respond to God's leading and become the persons we are called to be, doing what God calls us to do? No matter the circumstances, we have a choice to respond.

Esther 4:14 (underlining mine)

"14 For if you remain silent at this time, relief and deliverance for the Jews will arise from another place, but you and your father's family will perish. <u>And who knows but that you have come to your royal position for such a time as this</u>?"

The time for building a better you, following the example of God and the Two Great Commandments, is now. (Matthew 22:37-40) You may not have a "royal" position, but it's your *personal* position and opportunity. The time for telling truth and setting a godly example to help others become better, is now. This *is* the time, *here* is the place. How will you embrace the opportunity and the responsibility?

Early Years

My birth order, being a part of a large family in a small house with one bathroom, spending six years in a one room schoolhouse, being in a relationship since age sixteen, have required me to think about more than just my needs; I consider and include the needs of others.

The foundation for the bedrock truths in my life started in these early years but became a way of living throughout life.

The benefits from implementing the bedrock truths can be obtained by any person, in any situation, at any time.

I may have experienced some life situations that supported the bedrock truths early in my development, but there is no time like the present to build a better us starting with our relationship with God and applying the bedrock truths regularly.

Talk about a unique birth order! I was the youngest of seven children with six older sisters. My parents birthed a girl, then another girl, then twin girls! I would have quit there. Then another baby girl came along, and another, before they would have their baby boy, me. I was born in the small town of Custer, South Dakota. The news of the Hendrickson's finally getting a boy after six girls made the weekly paper!

Being the youngest of seven and the only boy, I spent a lot of time by myself. I had a few friends, but living in the country meant neighbors were fewer and farther away. Much of my time included riding my bike, hunting rabbits, birds, and squirrels with my .22, and fishing in the local lakes.

TV was not much of a draw for me as we only had one channel and in the summer the reception was not that good. I remember when we got a second channel. The stress of trying to manage viewing on *two* channels was new.

For grade school, I went to a one room school house where all my sisters had also attended; my dad and aunts and uncles had gone there, too. When I completed 6th grade, there had been 50 continuous years of Hendrickson's at the 4-Mile School.

To make recess engaging for a group of fifteen to twenty-five 1st through 6th graders was a challenge. All the students had a job, and the jobs changed as students grew older. For example, chalk board erasers were cleaned by the youngest, chalk boards were wiped down each day by other students, the flag was put up and taken down daily by older kids, and the flag was always folded properly at the end of the day. Water was gathered from the hand pump well, and the floors were swept each day. All the students pitched in.

My parents got divorced in the summer leading into the 6th grade. I was fortunate and given the choice of which parent I would live with. For the sake of less change, I stayed with my father and finished out grade school at the country school.

Junior High was a big change for me since all my classmates were the same age and there were many more of them. A student moved from class to class instead of staying at one desk all day as was done in the one room school house.

Junior High was the first time I got to play organized team sports, and I was a man among boys. In 7th grade, my height was 5'-10" and weight was 155 pounds. I was as tall as my coach! I played football, basketball, and threw the shot and discus. In football, I ran over people; in basketball, I got heckled by fans as they thought I was older and dumber than I was. They would say, "Pick on someone your own age!"

Actually, I was a very good student; I just had sideburns at an early age. I was known throughout the area for how far I could throw the discus, and always won first place. I still remember when a little guy came up to me and asked, "Are you Bud Hendrickson from Custer?" I answered, "Yes." His teammate was from Rapid City South and he told me he was going to kick my @#$ in the discus that day. That day, not only did I win, but set a new regional meet record!

Another big milestone during my Junior High days was that in South Dakota, when you turned fourteen, you could get a restricted license that allowed you to drive alone from 6 a.m. to 7 p.m. The first Friday after my 14th birthday, my dad took me down to the DMV to take the driver's test. I passed and was driving myself to school in 8th grade in a 1966 Blue Ford 4x4 pickup with no radio, affectionately called *Old Blue* by my family.

My high school would be considered quite small by some since it educated less than 300 students, 9th through 12th grade and I graduated in a class of 69 students. I didn't grow as tall or big as I thought I was going to; in my senior year I was about 6' 1" ad 195 pounds.

Football was my primary sport, but I still played basketball and threw the discus. I didn't dominate as much as I did in Junior High; I had to play smart in basketball being a 6'1" post player. I learned about position and using your body to your advantage! I ended my high school career winning the state discus championship as an underdog.

I was a good student in high school even though I was not planning on going to college. For some crazy reason,

I was good in math and enjoyed it, so I took advanced math and science all through high school.

It was my sophomore year that I asked Nancy Bradeen to the homecoming dance. The next week I asked her to go for a motorcycle ride. What I didn't know was that her father hated motorcycles and told Nancy's brothers that if they ever brought a motorcycle home, he would cut it up with a cutting torch. They were amazed he didn't say anything to me and allow his darling daughter to ride off on a motorcycle with that Hendrickson kid!

My dad co-signed a loan so I could buy the one and only new vehicle I would acquire in my entire life at the age of fourteen! I loved riding in the Black Hills with the wind in my face. I loved it so much that I would ride it to school even after the frosty weather hit the Hills.

After a few weekends of doing things with Nancy, no one would even ask her out, even though we had not officially stated we were dating. One year turned into two. We ended up serving as prom servers together our sophomore year, and attended Junior and Senior prom together.

Later in the book I go into more detail about how I ended up going to college and where, but a defining moment occurred shortly after starting college. I was attending the South Dakota School of Mines and Technology studying

Mechanical Engineering and playing football. Nancy had decided to attend Black Hills State College about 50 miles away; she was a cheerleader, and actually cheered against me when our colleges played each other!

Nancy had hinted she wanted a commitment, but I didn't want to get married until after college. We decided we could date other people while we were at college. I remember one day I was anxious about Nancy and me. My stomach was in knots and I was stressing out about our relationship. I got the Bible out that I had been given from our family church when I graduated. One verse highlighted on love on the front cover was I Corinthians 13. I opened up the Bible and as I read it, a sense of peace came over me. God did not use literal, audible words, but what He put on my mind was this: if our relationship was meant to be, she will be there for you. If she is not there, then she was not intended for you. I had never before had stress leave my body so completely or quickly.

Nancy had a few more dates than I did; I had only one. What this time did was to confirm to both of us we were the ones for each other. We ended up getting married at the end of my Junior year, 1987.

A blessing we experienced by being married was that all of life's challenges of finishing up college and choosing what job offer to accept, we embraced fully, considering the needs of both of us. Shortly after graduation, we packed up all our belongings and moved 1,000 miles east to Joliet, Illinois. That was a whole new world for us with no family or friends nearby. We were not only husband and wife, but best friends, and we did everything together.

Nancy and I were married about five years and we talked about starting a family. Like any couple, we started planning the next stage of life having children. We wanted to start the family after our ten-year class reunion. God had another plan, and we went back to our class reunion with a three-month-old named Grant! Nancy then thought it would be best to have the children five years apart so the second child would arrive about the time the first one started school, providing plenty of time to spend with the new child one-on-one. Of course, we wanted a girl so we would have one of each.

Brett, our second boy, arrived just twenty-one months after Grant! We would discover that there were benefits of having them closer together, but more importantly we came to realize the pros and cons with all birth orders, time in between, boys and girls, etc.

The key was to make the most of the kids, the timing, and order we had! I have enjoyed an empty nest as short as it was before Nancy died, but even her health challenges brought unique blessings with friends and family. I keenly observed how our relationships grew differently during this challenging time.

We had very few regrets and that is what **The Ten Bedrock Truths** are all about, having few regrets as you walk through life.

> I keenly observed how our relationships grew differently during this challenging time. We had very few regrets and that is what **The Ten Bedrock Truths** are all about, <u>having few regrets as you walk through life.</u>

Hit the Deck

After I wrote the book in 2016, life events kept unfolding and I learned how the Bedrock Truths were as effective in contemporary application as they were when I had used them earlier.

Literally just a few weeks after the book was published, I was working on upgrading the deck on my house. I had purchased the house in 2014, knowing that deck work was in the future. I wanted to replace the 2x6 decking material with plywood and a roof membrane. The deck was ten feet in the air and did not feel very stable, so we were planning on making improvements that required the deck joist brackets to be removed (we wanted to do double joists to give more support). This change would add additional screw points and overlap to the plywood as well.

The redesign also allowed us to move the joist higher up next to the house to get more slope for drainage. We had been working on the deck a few days and we ended the week with all the decking material off, and two of the joists doubled up and completed. We left the work with three joists hanging without brackets with a sheet of plywood over the top.

On a Sunday, I had some guests over to the house; we were eating, and drinking some wine. I went out on the deck and was standing on the plywood to show the progress and changes we were making. I don't know what happened then, but the plywood must have come off the joist causing me to fall ten feet onto the ground. The next thing I remember was my neighbor bending over me asking, "How are you doing?" I then remember talking to two EMTs, but don't remember them getting me onto the gurney, or into the ambulance, or the ride to the hospital.

The next thing I recall: I was at the hospital with medical professionals and my younger son, Brett, was talking to them. They were concerned that I had suffered a concussion, so Brett asked me, "Dad, what is the square root of 169?" I replied really quickly, "Thirteen," and they all laughed!

All I can tell you is that in sports I had played up through three years of college football and had never felt this beat up. My entire right side was bruised and broken: I had ten fractures in seven ribs, and a broken collar bone.

When a friend and Brett went back to the job site, they found my wine glass in one piece and with wine still in it. I must have had it in my left hand when all the damage occurred to my right side!

I spent two nights in the hospital and every time they asked me to sit up, get out of bed, or walk, tears came to my eyes. It was a huge emotional and physical effort to do any of these actions. When I came home, I could not sleep in the bed and getting out was hard, so I tried to sleep on the couch in a reclined position. It was better but the back wasn't tall enough to support my head. My sister brought over her large recliner and that was an improvement, but I still didn't sleep well with the pain. On top of all that, at the same time, I was out of work and looking for a job!

I spent much time contemplating the crazy situation in which I found myself. It would have been easy to look through the rear-view mirror and tear myself up that I even would have gone out there onto the unfinished deck. My friend was already being hard on himself as he could have easily put a 2x4 under the joists to better support the plywood platform we had made.

I chose to apply Bedrock Truth #10 and not beat myself up about what I could have done differently since it already had happened, but I asked myself, "How will I learn and grow from this unfortunate situation to build a better me?"

Though I was isolated and was not able to do much for a couple of months, I was getting better, and I had an end in sight. I hurt so badly and knew that I would never put myself in a position like that again. What I can tell you is this: I gained much empathy for people who had chronic health issues which brought them pain and mobility issues throughout life. Then I was reminded of the passion people dedicated to extreme sports had: like motocross, speed skiing, trick snowboarding, and rodeo. They would get as beat up as I was, or worse, and their plan was to get back at their sport as quickly as possible. What amazing strength and determination!

This recovery challenge allowed me to reflect on the courage and strength Nancy had shown in dealing with her cancer and chemotherapy for eighteen months. Her health had declined over that time and death was quickly approaching. How scary that must have been for her and how amazing the strength and courage it took to stare death in the face, live life, and invest in the people around her, regardless. If she could face that challenge, dealing with this painful setback seemed more doable.

Nancy passed away August 12, 2015, three days before our 28th anniversary.

*****

Meeting, Dating, and Marrying Kristin

After Nancy's passing, in August of 2015, I knew that I needed time to grieve but would someday meet someone and get remarried. When I felt ready to date again, I was hoping to meet someone in my network, but that network was in California. Since I had been living in Washington for almost three years, I decided to dip my toes into online dating.

It was during Memorial Day Weekend of 2017 that I decided I was going to try online dating for one month. I chose *Christian Mingle* since I knew I wanted to meet someone who had faith in God and who centered her life around Him. I have to admit looking at profiles was quite fascinating as to their interests and hobbies, and whether they were divorced, widowed, single and never married even in their late 40s and 50s!

I observed Kristin's profile. She liked to golf, ski, and dance. I thought to myself, "I used to golf and ski and enjoyed both, and I could learn to dance." She lived in Vancouver, Washington, which was close.

I sent a message to her indicating my interest to meet, and she accepted an invitation for dinner for June 14th, at a restaurant in quaint downtown Camas, Washington. I later found out that this date was my parent's wedding date and also my grandparents on my mother's side wedding date! Was this coincidence or providential?

I got to the restaurant early and picked out an outside seat to enjoy the beautiful evening and be somewhat private. I watched her drive up with a big smile on her face, and wave as she drove by to find parking. We had a great evening of conversation and closed the place down. Since she had to park some distance away, I offered to give her a ride to her car in my convertible. As I was driving down the backstreet to her car, I punched the accelerator and she lifted her hands up and smiled. She asked me if we could go for a drive. We went for that drive and didn't get her back to her car until about 11:30 p.m. on a work night. I can say this: dating is much different in your 50's than in your 20's as we were both very tired the next day at work.

I enjoyed my time immensely with Kristin, so wanting to be purposeful in my dating, I asked her how she liked to be pursued. I really feel it was important to share expectations so that there is no guesswork or situations where expectations are not met, unknowingly.

...it is important to share expectations so that there is no guesswork or situations where expectations are not met, unknowingly.

Within our first month of dating, Kristin was rear-ended on her way to work and her car was totaled. In a couple of our conversations, she had mentioned her desire to get a larger car as she felt vulnerable in the small car in traffic. Being a car guy, I started to look for a hybrid SUV like mine, and I found one! With the physical pain Kristin was enduring, and given all the other details she was working on, the last thing she wanted to do was look for a car.

We went together and looked at the car I had found, and she fell in love with the SUV. It had all the bells and whistles, All-Wheel Drive (AWD), leather seats, and a sunroof! Kristin was excited as she had never had a car with leather and a sunroof. After making the deal we went out for dinner and I asked her if we could be exclusive in our dating relationship, dating only each other, and she agreed.

We continued to be purposeful in our relationship by attending church together. It wasn't long before her mother, who was recovering from open heart surgery and could no longer drive, wanted to go back to church. Kristin and I made the collective decision to leave our churches in order to take her mother to her home church. What a great choice that was: to worship together, take her mom out for lunches, and of course, enjoy convertible car drives after church; these were added bonuses.

Many other purposeful choices about our relationship were discussed including not to have sex before marriage and not to move in with each other. In today's world, those choices seem foreign to most people. It may not be not easy, but putting God in the middle of a relationship requires this standard and there are blessings 100-fold when people follow and practice God's ways and commandments.

Forcing discipline in life is not a bad thing. Waiting for God's will and His way, also keeps the focus on being "on-purpose" and making good decisions regarding the relationship. These include the decision to get married in a timely thought-out manner.

> Forcing discipline in life is not a bad thing.

For our wedding, we wanted a message that honestly represented what our marriage union was about. Upon searching, we came across **Ecclesiastes 4:12**:

> Though one may be overpowered, two can defend themselves. A cord of three strands is not quickly broken.

In our wedding ceremony, we had three cords tied to a gold ring. One cord was gold, the other purple, the third one, white. The gold cord represented the Divinity of God, the covenant relationship initiated by Him and built under His authority, and was intended to glorify Him. The purple cord represented the groom and as Christ loved the church, the husband loving his wife and submitting himself to the Lord. The bride's purity was represented by the white cord as the wife honors her husband and submits herself to the Lord.

God, in turn, then nurtures and strengthens the marriage relationship. During the marriage ceremony, I held the ring while Kristin took the cords and braided them together with the gold cord always in the middle and the purple cord (groom) and white cord (bride) wrapped around this gold cord representing God. This made for a *stronger* cord that was not easily broken!

I was also reminded that our relationship is like a triangle. God is at the top and the husband and wife are at the bottom corners. The closer we get to God, the closer we get to each other!

Getting married the second time is not perfect since there are two imperfect people coming together. But with God at the center of our marriage, we are stronger, and able to work through issues and life events *together* and build a better us in the process!

> ... with God at the center of our marriage, we are stronger, and able to work through issues and life events *together* and build a better us in the process!

The key component in a good marriage is this: it is to be lived out with the acronym HELP. This relationship concept is explained in **The Enduring Foundation for Change** * *Ten to One Relationships,* page 151.

Remember this fact: Cutting corners doesn't get you where you want to be faster or better.

> Remember this fact: Cutting corners doesn't get you
> where you want to be faster or better.

Building a Safe Environment Is Part of Building a Better You

I concluded it is more important to have my home be a safe environment for people, even the ones I may not see eye to eye with. In one instance, surrounding a political discussion, it got kind of heated. Following our discussion, which really was an argument, I reached out and apologized in person when I needed to, for disagreeing and possibly offending a neighbor. I owned my actions, asked for forgiveness, and requested nothing in return.

It freed my soul up and also got me to reevaluate this maxim: always trying to win an argument is not the best action and I concluded how important it is to focus more on the people in front of us than the politicians in Washington, D.C. and elsewhere whom we probably will never meet.

A political argument is child's play compared to the environment in which we live today with COVID-19, volatility, riots, economic upheaval, election controversies, Big Tech censorship, media coverage, and cancel culture.

Find Common Ground

When other people feel left out, neglected, don't have God or a supportive spouse, a solid foundation to work from, what a burden they must be carrying!

Finding common ground (mutual understanding) is a topic I wrote about in *God's Plan Unfolding * Strength and Renewal in Times of Crisis* (www.godsplanunfolding.com). This precept is more important than ever in our current world.

> From the book, used by permission of Glen Aubrey, Creative Team Publishing, and Bud Hendrickson, Contributor (pages 121-122):
>
> "How do we find Common Ground and Mutual Understanding in divisive times?" Name-calling and looking through the rearview mirror to find fault are not the answers, yet we see wrong answers play out every day on multiple media channels and possibly in our real lives, too, no matter the crisis. We need to look through the rearview mirror to celebrate accomplishments or learn

from past actions/results that will allow us to look through the windshield to better navigate through these challenging issues moving forward.

Finding common ground requires us to reach out to people with other perspectives and expertise, to find out the real issues they are confronting and what their ideas are for dealing with the challenges. Then, coming from their perspectives, can we find areas of common needs and benefits where we can share from our experience and expertise the actions and solutions we may consider? *With identified common ground hopefully there is trust and respect that will allow conversation to continue.*

As Christians, let's ask: "Are we willing to look into someone else's world where there may be effective actions different from our own?" "Will we be willing to be open to conversations that could form the catalyst that allows even more powerful and effective solutions to emerge?" If we can consider these options, imagine the trust and strength of relationships that could be built providing foundations upon which to build even more successes in dealing with the issues that lie ahead for all of us!

To be honest, I *need* to find common ground and mutual understanding with those with whom I deal. My linebacker mentality wants to kick butt and take names. That action, however, isn't the most effective way to encourage and get others on a firmer foundation for living so they can make better decisions and become more effective in their lives.

If All Would Follow The Ten Bedrock Truths

If all would follow **The Ten Bedrock Truths**, what a different world we would live in. Human nature hasn't changed since Adam and Eve; just the names, times, and situations are different. I find it amazing how so many in our world want to blame someone else for their own problems.

We need to ask the question: "Who can make the best decisions for your life?" You? Government? The whole idea of this book is the value of making more informed, better decisions for you, because only you have control over your own personal behavior and actions. You have the most information and knowledge about your interests and needs, and you alone possess the motivation to act on them.

Upon reading up on our Founding Fathers, I came across some things to consider as we strive to build a better me and a better you. The 55 Founding Fathers took six weeks during a hot, Philadelphia summer in 1787 to draft the preamble to the constitution. It was only 52 words in length, but set the foundation of what we would call 'a vision statement' today for the development of the laws to govern the new country.

There is much debate regarding the faith of the Founding Fathers, but one thing that stands out is they didn't always believe the same Biblically as to the tenets of salvation, but *all* agreed Biblically when it came to structuring the new government of the new country, which we now call The United States of America.

In structuring the new government, the Founders were heavily influenced by a Biblical view of man and government. They understood the sinfulness of man which resulted in a system of government of limited authority in any one branch (Executive, Legislative, and Judicial), with numerous checks and balances. For this type of government to work, let me ask: "Is there a need for the citizens to have a moral or righteous foundation?"

From what I have read, I feel it is obvious: the importance of righteousness in its citizenry is required for this experiment in government to work. The events of the year 2020 have shown how division, name-calling, and lack of common ground have resulted in less than effective government and vast divisions in the people who are tasked with addressing the major issues at hand.

I would hope that *Enjoy Greater Results with Less Effort * Build a Better You* will allow improved and informed decisions to be made because of the improved relationships which develop. Superior information and confidence are obtained in the process.

In the application of **The Ten Bedrock Truths** on your journey, I am confident that a strong moral fiber within you will be strengthened. Hopefully, this strengthening will become a catalyst for others around you to do the same.

My prayer is that this would be the start of a more informed and righteous citizenry to help our government create the environment for exceptionalism in America again.

If we want the United States to be a "shining city on a hill" to the world, our country needs to be healthy and vibrant. May your efforts to build a better you be the spark that lights a fire of rebirth in your family which will spread to your neighborhood which can bring healing and health to our country!

In John Winthrop's sermon of 1630, he employed the phrase, "a city on a hill." He caused it to become the key statement that he most feared and lamented. In the years to come, Winthrop's "city upon a hill" sermon would become "the shining city on a hill" of President Ronald Reagan: a celebration of individual freedom, material prosperity, and

American power—above all, a call for Americans to renew their optimism and believe in themselves again.

Bedrock Truth #1

Change: An Opportunity or a Threat

My manager at my first job, after I had just completed college, was a great leader and exposed his team to new truths that expanded our paradigm. He was a Joel Barker fan, and in one of Joel's videos that the manager showed at a team building event, was this line I have lived with: "Change is either an opportunity or a threat and it is your choice." How true this is! Time after time I have seen this unfold in my life where change was an opportunity for me.

Change is an interesting word and it brings out different emotions from different people at different times in life. When I look back at my life, most of our big events in life were results of change. Getting married was one big change. And on our wedding day, true happiness came from that change. The birth of a child is another big change. And again, what joy came from that big change.

Let's look at change from a technology standpoint. Would you still want the quality of picture and size of TV you watched when you were young? In my lifetime I have gone from an 8-track tape, cassette tape, CD, and now digital music from a phone or storage device. The quality and the ability to move around and choose the song you want to hear is so much better today. How about cell phones? Are you glad we have them and have you benefitted from the advancement of the cell phone, where you can do almost anything on them?

I like to look at cars and the changes in them and how much better they are today. When I grew up, all cars were carbureted. I lived at a 5300-ft. elevation so the carburetor would have to be adjusted for that elevation, and when it was adjusted, the car ran fine. When the car would be driven to Rapid City, which was about a 3200-ft. elevation, it would idle high and run much differently. Make a drive to Colorado and drive up to a 10,000-ft. elevation, and it ran terribly and had no power.

Today the fuel injected car monitors and makes adjustments to maximize the performance at all elevations and operating conditions. The safety features in the cars of today are staggering versus the cars of 30 years ago. My Boss Mustang reminds me of the love-hate relationship I have with old cars. The history with them is interesting and the car's styling was so distinctive that if you knew what to look for you could identify make, model, and year of each car. But for drivability, safety, and reliability, I will take a newer car with all the modern conveniences any day!

The other side of not changing or changing fast enough is being forced into obsolescence. In my life one of the most recognizable brand names was Kodak ™ and they dominated the film camera and paper market. (KODAK is a trademark of Eastman Kodak Company.) Everyone knew the name Kodak and the quality of products they had for photography. In 1975 a Kodak engineer developed and patented the first digital camera. Kodak was already successful and they did not jump onto the digital photography tidal wave. According to their reasoning, this change was not in alignment with the success they had experienced from their past*. Other companies like Canon, Nikon, Pentax, and Panasonic took the opportunity to expand the market and grow with the change. How many people under the age of twenty even know what Kodak is?
*http://www.ipwatchdog.com/2014/11/01/the-rise-and-fall-of-the-company-that-invented-digital-cameras/id=51953/

When it comes to our careers, businesses, or life journeys, do we want to be a Kodak of the 1970s and not embrace change and miss the opportunity to grow and become better? Or do we want to embrace change as it comes and look for opportunities for growth and improvement that the change will provide? Do we want film cameras or digital cameras that are so small that they fit in our cell phones and we can take pictures all the time and wherever we are? Do we want to wait to see the picture when it is developed, or do we want to view it instantly and take another picture if we don't like the picture we just took?

Why do we view change so negatively much of the time when it comes to our lives? Is it because we are comfortable and that comfort is more important than learning and growing from the change that is going to occur? Do we feel threatened that a weakness will be exposed, or does doubt creep in when that which made us successful in the past is changing?

Change is a part of the events in all of our lives. Some changes we have control over, but many come our way whether we like them or not. Change is neither good nor bad, but how we embrace it and grow from it will determine how it impacts our lives. If we reject change, the results may treat us poorly. Joy may be minimized and negativity can creep into our life. Many times, if you resist change in your work, your performance will suffer. Many people lose their jobs because they are no longer in alignment with the direction of the organization. But if you embrace change, you can maximize the opportunity the change offers to bring to your life. You will grow, learn, and meet the needs of *why* the change was initiated in the first place. Most of the time the negative effects of the change won't occur, and there are positives that were never seen or considered at the beginning of the change.

When change appears, it can be uncomfortable and complicated. Times of change, however, should be times where we are open and ask for perspectives from diverse people who may not think like us. In these times much insight can be obtained to address and incorporate change as effectively as possible. (This topic will be covered in more detail in Chapter 7, The Power of Diversity.)

This small group of diverse people could be the support system needed to deal with the emotions that come when dealing with the challenges of change. This small group may also give insight on how to plan for the successes that lie ahead because of dealing with change effectively.

Let's face it, embracing change doesn't have to mean "comfort" or complete acceptance at first. When opportunities for growth do come along, the person who wants to build a better version of themselves will likely benefit from looking carefully at new options and weighing them before deciding to reject any new ideas and remaining stuck in the old ways of learning and doing.

Personal growth can be maximized and opportunities can come from situations we never thought possible. Is change an opportunity or threat? It's your choice, so make the most of it!

> If you embrace change, you can maximize the opportunity the change offers, to bring greater results to your life with less effort.

Review and Respond

1. What changes in your life or career have you embraced that brought about positive results?

_____

_____

_____

_____

_____

2. What kinds of resistance or negative emotions do you experience when new opportunities are presented to you?

_____

_____

_____

_____

_____

3. What actions accompany your choices to embrace the changes you deem are good for you?

_____

_____

_____

_____

_____

4. How can you improve your processes of evaluation when changes are presented for you to consider?

_____

_____

_____

_____

_____

_____

_____

Bedrock Truth #2

Margin: Time and Money

We hear the word "margin" all the time. As you read this book you are benefiting from how the publisher provides a margin around the perimeter of the type. Did you know that about 40% of the page is margin? You may ask, "Why would they 'waste' so much of the page and not save money and print on fewer pages?" The reason is that your enjoyment would go way down since the book would be much more difficult to read.

I have experienced that when I have allowed or provided no margin with my time and money, my stress level grows exponentially and that condition robs me of so much enjoyment on my journey. In 2014 I received a phone call at work that lasted longer than I expected it to and I got on the road to the airport with no time to spare. To make my day, an accident occurred and the traffic was very slow as I headed toward the airport. I just watched my watch tick on by as my stress continued to climb. In my mind I was thinking of what I would do if I missed my plane and all the events this missed flight would affect. Fortunately, this story ended well and I got to the gate just as the boarding process concluded, but many circumstances like this do not end well, and the stress and loss of enjoyment continue.

Have you ever experienced an event like this? How much enjoyment was robbed from your day or that part of your journey?

Consider these scenarios:

1. You are late for work and this occurrence puts you over the point count and you stand to be disciplined or fired. While I have seen this scenario play out many times, the reality is that a person usually doesn't get fired for being late just once. To get fired this pattern is repeated numerous times and is probably a result of not providing enough margin in travel time to work.
2. How about being over committed, where you feel you cannot keep up with the workload or you need to be in two places at one time?

These margin issues with time can cause high levels of stress and rob you of your enjoyment. Prioritizing what is important to you and allocating proper time for these priorities can give you the space to choose better, and enjoy the processes more.

Not providing enough margin with regard to finances is another area that can cause your stress levels to rise to high levels. A key lesson here is that providing sufficient margin in finances is not a function of whether you make enough money. It is a function of whether you spend more money than you have. It is amazing that 44% of lottery winners who win millions of dollars end up penniless within 5 years. Over half of professional athletes after making millions find themselves in the same situation and go bankrupt. (http://www.sfgate.com/business/article/How-stars-so-rich-and-famous-can-go-broke-3226082.php)

The primary issue with the people who make a lot of money and who do not have sufficient margin with their finances is that there are more 0s in their debt number.

When I graduated from college, many of the car dealers parked brand-new cars in front of our student union building to entice soon-to-be-graduating engineers into buying a new car. These dealers even postponed the payments until after the engineer started the job. Not me. I purchased a 4-year-old pickup for about half the price of a new one. I can say that I have never bought a new car in my entire life. They have typically been one to six years old, but boy did I save a lot of money over the years in depreciation of my cars. Where I spent my money instead was restoring my high school car, a 1969 Boss 302 Mustang that my wife and I drove to our prom. That was a bigger priority to me than driving a new car that people would put door dings in while it was in a parking lot.

Another reason we chose to buy used cars is that my wife and I made a decision that she would be a full-time manager of the house to raise our children. She worked as an office manager up to the day our first son was born. With the loss in income, we had to make choices of how and where we spent our money. When we would eat out on many of our activities as a family, we would drink water instead of getting a drink. It is amazing how much money it costs to have the soda, beer, and wine. It was more important to have good food than drinks, and we didn't need the carbs, either. But it was another choice we made to help our money go farther. Our boys practice ordering water with their meals today in their young adult years.

Whenever my employer would match any money that I would contribute into a retirement account, there was no question that I would participate. Years ago, my employer would match 1% of my pay if I saved for a retiree medical savings plan. I was in. I would not even miss 1% of my pay. What was amazing is that years later when my wife was diagnosed with cancer and I was unemployed and paying $1,700 a month in COBRA (Consolidated Omnibus Budget Reconciliation Act) insurance premiums and maximizing the out-of-pocket expenses of the insurance plan, I was able to use this account for these expenses. Without that unexpected fund to tap into, our finances would have become a disaster and our stress meter would have pegged out. When I started saving into this account, I would never have guessed it would be used for an emergency like I was facing. That unintentional action I took many years earlier paid big dividends in a crucial moment in our lives. That savings account gave us the margin we needed in a life moment we could have never thought or believed would happen to us.

Sometimes it is good to evaluate where we are spending our money, to ensure it is still important or a priority. In 2010 I evaluated the need for a boat we had enjoyed for ten years. Up until the last couple of years, we had used the boat regularly, but then we started using it only two or three times a year. I calculated it would cost me less to rent the boat for those outings than what it cost to insure and maintain the boat every year. The boat was very reliable for the ten years we had it, but the boat and trailer also needed some work done and that was going to cost some money. So like the old saying goes, the two best days for a boat owner is the day they bring it home and the day they sell it. Even though we had many great memories on that boat, I looked forward to the money saved and seeing the work and effort to maintain the boat going away.

Another decision I made about our finances was selling our 1969 Mustang GT Convertible. Nancy and I bought the car in 1992 BC (before children), and it was a lot of fun. We also thought it was neat we could give each of our boys a car later in life. But by 2013, the interior was cracking badly, the brake master cylinder had gone out, the power steering cylinder was leaking, and we had a fuel leak. The car was one of 151 with the engine and transmission code and it really needed to be restored properly. I did not want to spend that kind of money as I had done it once, and neither of my boys would be able to spend the money for years, if ever. I listed it, was patient, and found the right buyer for the car who was going to restore it to its former glory. Again, I not only put money in the bank, but eliminated the annual insurance and license costs. These two decisions increased the margin in our finances that would benefit us later at a time when trying to make those same decisions would have been very difficult as we dealt with my wife's health issue while I was busy in a job search.

How are your margins with your time and money? Is your stress higher than it needs to be and stealing joy from your life? Have you ever prioritized your time and spending, to ensure you are spending your time and resources on the most important things in your life? Are all your needs getting addressed, or are your wants getting in the way and causing you to spend too much or all of your money and leaving no funds in savings as a margin for an unexpected life event?

How are your margins with your time and money?
Is your stress higher than it needs to be and stealing joy
from your life?

Review and Respond

1. The act of providing margins for time and money is not accidental. It's intentional. What changes would you consider making to start allocating sufficient margins in your time and money?

_____

_____

_____

_____

2. What are the primary causes of stress in your life? How many of those stress factors are related to insufficient margins?

_____

_____

_____

_____

_____

3. Providing margins takes discipline. Discipline is one of the hallmarks of balanced people, and of those who are prepared for the unexpected. How disciplined are you?

_____

_____

_____

_____

_____

_____

4. What other areas besides time and money would be areas in which you should have more margin?

_____

_____

_____

_____

_____

_____

Bedrock Truth #3

Opportunity Is Missed by Most

My father was a product of the depression and I joke that I am also, but people say I am too young. This is true, but important values do get passed on and the emphasis of hard work and wasting nothing is a part of my fabric. This is why this quote by Thomas Edison hits home with me: "Opportunity is missed by most because it is dressed in overalls and looks like work."

Just to give you an insight as to what a person from the depression would do to save money and be independent:

> When we would go deer hunting, most hunters would take the prime cuts and throw the rest away. My dad cut every last piece of meat away and we even sawed up the rib bones and they would be boiled to make venison and noodle soup. You grow a garden and even the turnip greens are eaten. We had a 1966 Ford pickup we affectionately called the Blue Bomb. All the kids learned to drive in it. It had no AC, no power steering, and not even an

AM radio! In 1976 my dad splurged and got an
AM radio in his pickup. Now that was
something!

Growing up I never got an allowance as a means to get
money. I had certain jobs that I had to do as a part of my
responsibility, like mowing the grass, splitting wood, and
keeping the wood box filled up during the winter. To earn
money, I had to work in the family wood preservative
business. From grade school I worked in the summer from
7:30 a.m. to 5:00 p.m. around adults in an industrial
environment, taking bark off the timber, grading to size,
trimming length, and banding them into similar sized
bundles. I got a fair wage and was even paid overtime, so
I earned a lot of money for someone my age.

One of our side businesses was delivering the treated
posts and poles throughout the region. To take advantage of
the drive back, my dad would purchase hay for a backhaul
home. We sold some of the hay in truckload quantities and
we also sold some by the bale to horse owners in the area.
So, on a cold winter evening when someone stopped by to
pick up ten bales of hay, guess who got to go load it? You
got it, me! I was not a happy camper at the time, but as I
look back, this composed many of the building blocks that
made up my work ethic.

As I was entering my junior year of high school, it was
obvious the business was not going to last. Cheaper

products from Canada were available, and the real dagger to the company was that the treatment chemical we used had been classified as a carcinogen and was being taken off the market. My first career choice of taking over the family business was going away.

My dad had a conversation about what I was planning to do after high school and I thought I would become a machinist or welder. My dad just looked me in the eyes and said, "I have seven children and I don't have a college graduate." The crazy thing is that even though I hadn't planned on going to college out of high school, I had taken the math and science classes offered because I was good at it and enjoyed them. The closest college was South Dakota School of Mines and Technology, 40 miles away, which was the best engineering college in the state and was a state college that would be more cost effective.

After I had made my decision, another profound comment came from my father. He said, "I am not in a position to help you with college, so you will have to pay for it with what you can earn in the summer and borrow in student loans. You will not use grant money because that is a handout from the government." You don't hear that kind of talk much anymore but it was commonplace for a self-made person who took pride in being self-sufficient and responsible for his actions and outcomes.

The opening day at the School of Mines found us in the gymnasium for orientation. I will never forget the first presenter talking about the excellence and hard work that was required to make it at the School of Mines. The presenter said look to your left and now look to your right. At the end of four years, one of the three of you will be left. Boy, was *that* a motivator!

To add to the motivation, my American College Testing (ACT) score results included valuable information at the bottom, like, "What is the likelihood you will maintain a C average at the school of your choices?" At the School of Mines there was less than a 50% chance of maintaining a C average. I asked myself, "What was I getting into?"

The first semester was a real challenge. The workload was much larger than I had had in high school. During the week, I felt like the water level was getting above my nose and I was drowning in work. During the weekend I would work hard and I felt like I got the water level just below my nose so we could start it all over again the next week.

The class that presented the biggest challenge was calculus. It was like another language and the concepts were so foreign to me. My grade was suffering and I actually had to drop the class. I ended the first semester with a 3.0 Grade Point Average (GPA) and I started to get confidence that I could make it here! I retook Calculus, passed it the next semester, and ended up taking five more advanced math classes before I graduated.

During the first semester of my third year, I was studying for a big test in a duplex I shared with three roommates. One of my roommates was on the phone for a long time. When he hung up, he said, "The phone is going to ring and it is going to be for you, Bud." What I did not know or could even expect was that the operator had broken into his call and told him there was an important call for Bud Hendrickson and that he needed to hang up. It was my aunt calling to inform me that my dad had died. What a shock that was, and I even said, "You are joking, right?" She had to inform me that she was not and that it had happened suddenly while he was at home watching the Monday Night Football game after eating dinner.

Many of you may be able to relate to this. In a time of stress and great loss, you can't sleep, it's hard to think and make decisions, and rollercoaster emotions come out of nowhere. I lived five days of these kinds of emotional ups and downs before I had to get back to college and into the swing of things.

It was actually good to get back into a routine again. And I will always remember the thoughts my father shared when I was a young child and I saw him cry for the first time after his mother passed. He shared how important it was to live life. We honor those who die by how we live our lives, honoring their legacy and what was important to them. Now I had to move on and live life, this was my opportunity to make my dad proud while I fulfilled my goals!

As I entered into higher-level classes that made up my major in Mechanical Engineering, my grades took off as I started to see how all this math had a purpose and place and would be applied to solve problems. I ended up graduating with a 3.59 GPA, far from the C average I had a 50% chance of obtaining, and yes, was one of the three to make it through the four years and graduate. There were students that were smarter than me, but I had the focus and diligent work ethic to navigate through the tough times and challenges along the way.

Choices emerged from this hard work when it came to employers. With a lot of guidance and prayer, I chose a company that gave me a great opportunity to experience exemplary leadership and teamwork in action, and that was a foundation upon which I would build my career.

> "Opportunity is missed by most because it is dressed in overalls and looks like work." ~ Thomas Edison

Do you have examples in your life or in the lives of others you know where hard work sets the way for opportunities? What kind of satisfaction do you feel after succeeding in a difficult task or situation? All I can say is this part of my journey gave me the confidence to address challenges head-on, not knowing the outcome, but giving it my best effort along the way.

What satisfaction I received, being successful in an arena in which I was told I would not achieve success. The only emptiness during this part of my journey was that my father was not there to see me walk and get my degree upon graduation. But he got his college graduate! And his college graduate was deeply grateful for the example his father had set!

As I reflect back on this part of my journey, I think about how much different my life would have been had I not appreciated my father's work ethic and values and applied them in my life. I saw how people in the community respected my father for his integrity and how he worked with people. My respect grew as I learned more about the person who lived through a very tough time in our country's history called the Depression. I learned to value the perspective of someone who not only has lived more life stages than I had, but also cared about my best interest as a person. I learned the value of wisdom, learning from someone else's mistakes versus the experience of learning only from your own mistakes.

I knew I was going to get enough experience anyway, so why not take advantage and get as much wisdom as possible from someone who has already lived through much of these same experiences? They say hindsight is 20/20, so why not take advantage of someone who has that hindsight in dealing with issues you are dealing with now?

Review and Respond

1. What are some of the values you treasure and upon which you face your challenges and make your choices?

   _____

   _____

   _____

   _____

   _____

2. How do you handle change, especially when it forces you to have to deal with new circumstances?

   _____

   _____

   _____

   _____

   _____

   _____

3. What places do guidance from friends and trusted counselors and prayer and trust in God have in your processes of making decisions?

_____

_____

_____

_____

_____

_____

_____

4. Why is working hard important, particularly when you are convinced that you are following the correct path of endeavor?

_____

_____

_____

_____

_____

_____

Bedrock Truth #4

Doing Your Best, Doing It Right

I have never been the most athletic, smartest, or experienced, but I have been able to compete both athletically and professionally with hard work and doing the right thing. I concluded that if I was to write a book, it would include this core thought: "Work hard while doing your best, do the right things, and go through the doors of opportunity that are in front of you."

So many times, I see people put that goal way "out there" and miss opportunities in front of them because they were *only* focused on the star so far removed. I did not have that paradigm growing up and it was a great ride along the way!

But I've been amazed and envy people who always knew what their passion was and what they wanted to do when they grew up. They were focused on aiming for the goal that was represented by the star in the sky.

I was an early developer and turned 18 just months into my senior year because my birthday was three weeks from the cutoff date. When I graduated from high school, I had no clue what I wanted to do and possessed no paradigm to know where to start with putting a star in the sky as a goal.

I have to chuckle when I see parents putting their children into school a year early because they are so smart or "ready." I look at the other end when they graduate at seventeen and they are one year less mature. I am glad my parents chose to wait to get me started in school.

Even though I didn't have a passion or "star in the sky" goal to chase, my work ethic and values originally demonstrated by my parents started a foundation of doing well in school. I worked hard and played fair on the playground and treated others with respect. In high school I took all the classes that were needed for college but did not plan on attending. When my door of opportunity closed on the family business, a door to attend college opened up.

In Chapter 3 I shared the work it took to make it through college while majoring in Mechanical Engineering. I had no idea what a Mechanical Engineer did because I had no role models in my life of anyone who were engineers, nor was I exposed to any work environments utilizing engineers.

After my father passed away in 1985 and during the fall semester of my junior year of college, I knew I had to figure out what I was going to do when I grew up. The next semester, during spring practice for football, I was moved from defensive line to offensive center because the starting center was going to graduate. This was the first time I was offered a scholarship to play football, but in my mind, I was still preoccupied with the thought, "What am I going to do when I graduate?"

As I was finishing up spring practice, a roommate of mine told me about some companies that were coming on campus to interview for internships. I signed up for a couple of interviews and a few weeks later I was offered an intern position in a maintenance department of a manufacturing company. I went up to my coach and told him I appreciated his investment in me and the challenge to play center. With the recent passing of my father, I told the coach I needed to find out what I am going to do after graduation. I shared with him that I got an internship that would require me to work during the summer and the fall semester. Even though coach hated to see me leave after all the investment he made in me during spring practice, he knew my motive was right and honored my decision.

If you haven't experienced it by now, the newest or lowest level person gets to do all the dirty, hard jobs. My internship was no different. I got to work in the hot and dusty raw material-conveying areas of the plant. Being of Scandinavian heritage, I love cool weather and when it is hot, I sweat, which allows my body to maintain a consistent temperature. The dust would stick to me and I was a wet mess. My boss and co-workers would even accuse me of throwing dust on myself to make it look like I was working! I worked hard and did my best to contribute during the seven months I worked on that internship. I received a great review and was offered to work there again the following summer.

In my senior year I spent most of my time interviewing and traveling to visit companies. There were numerous students with similar grades but the difference was this: I had work experience. My ability to talk to people and be relevant because of my work experiences set me apart during the interview process. I had about eight to ten offers to consider. The hardest part was choosing what job was the right one for me. What a great position to be in, and at the time I didn't even realize it. I ended up going with a company in Joliet, Illinois that was highly automated and fit my interests the most.

What I never knew when I chose this company was what a great manager I would have and the great team environment that was there. A new full-time engineer could not have asked for a better environment in which to grow and build a foundation for future success. This company is where I was exposed to "Change is either an opportunity or threat and it is your choice." This is also where I experienced the value of diverse skill sets as well as the value of using these skill sets to solve issues as effectively as possible. I also benefitted from the experience of a 30-year manufacturing veteran who, because of my respect for him and what he brought to the team, invested in me. Even though he did not have a degree, he had so much experience and knowledge that I could benefit from as a new and inexperienced engineer. As I worked with him and our trust developed, I welcomed opportunities to invest in him in the technology side which was my strength, and we made each other better team members for the company.

I had received an interview with a human resources (HR) director about five years into my career and was asked if I had any relocation restrictions. I replied that I had none; it would mean only a different airport to fly back to South Dakota for Christmas and family events. I did mention that if there was ever an opportunity in Colorado or California facilities, I would be interested because it would be closer to "home" and family.

About six months later an opportunity became available in Fresno, California, which the company invited me to consider. My wife and I moved to California when our oldest son was ten months old, and we drove three-quarters of the way across the country with my Boss Mustang riding on a trailer behind the moving truck.

The work environment in Fresno was much different than the one in Joliet. On my last job performance review in Joliet, a comment was placed at the end of the review that said, "Bud challenges the system and it leads to exciting results." In California, I ended up in an environment that did not want to be challenged to be better. I was told by peers, "We don't do things like that here." What did I get myself into with this move!? There were a handful of motivated employees that I gravitated toward and worked with as much as I could. Some structural changes were made and some of the "old guard" moved to other locations or retired. Working hard and tapping into the talent at the site resulted in some significant improvements. Company goals were being established that did not allow for just working harder, but required a new way of doing things to accomplish the business goals. This view provided an environment for my leadership and teamwork skills to take root and influence the site. Five years later, my first manager in Fresno was now working for me and so were all of my peers. Who would have ever thought that could happen?

Even though there were some professional challenges, the move to California was great for the family. The church we found ended up being a great place to grow spiritually. The community was a great place to raise our children and the schools were of high quality. Living four to seven hours away from many family members by car allowed us to invest in family relationships and participate in holiday events like Thanksgiving dinners in Vegas at my mother's place.

One of our family activities was snow skiing, and the High Sierra Mountains provided great opportunities for us to ski and snowboard throughout the years. We got spoiled with all the sunshine and warm weather, so for ten years we did a lot of boating on nearby lakes during the summer months.

When the company where I had worked for twenty-two years was shutting down the facility where I was employed, I made a choice to change companies and industries to be able to stay in the Fresno area. I made this decision so my oldest son who was a senior in high school and my younger son who was a sophomore didn't have to move. As much as I thought I had been a change agent, all of a sudden, because of circumstances and desires, I was making a tough decision, requiring a change for me to evaluate and act upon. I found myself experiencing anxiety because I was going to leave a position with which I had invested so much time and knew so well. To top it off, I was leaving a site that was highly automated and employed only 75 employees. Fifty-two of these employees operated the production lines with 39 not on site at any given time, because they were either part of the next shift or were on their days off.

My new company was a seasonal food manufacturer whose employee force would grow from 150 year-round employees to over 1,000 overnight for the seasonal harvest. The processes at this firm were not optimized like I was accustomed to, and the "seasonal" workforce had not seen or operated any machinery for nine months, or they were completely new and had no experience at all with the processes.

After two years my position was eliminated, but that change gave me the courage and confidence that taught me that I could make my situation work wherever I am!

So, my next job was with another seasonal food company where fruit was frozen. I was asked to reorganize the maintenance team. It was a great experience and I was exposed to ammonia refrigeration, which was new to me. Once the changes were implemented, my job again was eliminated and I was in the job market again!

Three months later is when my wife was diagnosed with cancer. I had been diligently working on the job search for about four months when I was contacted by a recruiter in January about an opportunity that required relocation. I told the recruiter that I was not interested in relocating but that I appreciated him considering me. I continued to look for work within an hour radius of where I lived. I started to look further and my endeavors were not finding opportunities that fit me. The recruiter contacted me again in April and I agreed to interview for the position. I flew up on a Tuesday to the Portland, Oregon area and interviewed on Wednesday. It went well so on Thursday I got a verbal offer and on Friday the written offer was sent to me.

I did not want to relocate from a community where we had lived for twenty years and that had supported us during the first months of my wife's battle with cancer. But the move and job turned out to be a blessing that we could never have imagined. During the first year we had 30 different visitors who came to visit us. Most of our guests drove 750 miles and some took an airplane ride from various states to visit. They stayed in our home where we had more one-on-one time to share personally. We got to explore the new area's sites and attractions with all our friends and family. The work is very rewarding and I get to work with great people. The job requires me to travel, but at my point in life it has been enjoyable. I don't live in the "forever-house" my wife and I built in 2004, but we ended up residing in a neighborhood that made us feel at home from the very beginning. Our new home provided a great view of the Columbia River and Mount Hood, and that panorama constantly reminds me of the provision that God has for us, greater than any we plan for or can even imagine.

I truly believe in the "Work hard while doing your best, do the right things, and go through the doors of opportunity that are in front of you" philosophy. Working hard may be pretty easy to put our minds around. But how about "do the right thing"? My definition of "do the right thing" is this: "Can you pass the 'red face test' if you share your motives and actions to all that are affected by what you do?" The "red face test" is not the same for all people, of course, but you need to worry only about *your* "red face test."

I can also say as I have matured spiritually and raised children, my "red face test" has evolved. There is much more that can make my face turn red due to my increase in sensitivity to what is and is not right in attitudes and actions.

Could I ever have planned my journey and the points of interest along the way? No way! For me, had I not been open to new ventures and worked hard at achieving them, I would have missed a great journey. Your journey could take you around the world. It could take you to places across the country like mine did. Or it could be a journey in the same town your entire life. No journey is better than another. The question is, are we enjoying our journey as much as we can? Are we positively impacting the people and situations over which we have influence along the way?

> Work hard while doing your best, do the right things,
> and go through the doors of opportunity
> that are in front of you.

Review and Respond

1. What is your "star" or goal you desire to achieve no matter what?

_____

_____

_____

_____

_____

2. How do strong work ethic and personal values contribute to achieving success regardless of where your journey takes you?

_____

_____

_____

_____

_____

_____

3. How valuable are the "uncomfortable" environments and how willing are you to experience them in order to gain new experiences and fresh perspectives toward achieving what you really desire?

_____

_____

_____

_____

_____

_____

_____

4. If a new environment diminishes or inhibits your creativity and contributions, what should you do?

_____

_____

_____

_____

_____

_____

5. In an environment when circumstances beyond your control force you to consider change, how do you weigh your options and upon what values and fundamental truths do you make your choices?

    _____

    _____

    _____

    _____

    _____

6. If you agree with the philosophy of "Work hard, do the right thing, and go through doors of opportunity that open to you," what does that philosophy look like in your life and experience?

    _____

    _____

    _____

    _____

    _____

    _____

Bedrock Truth #5

Ninety Percent for Today and Ten Percent for Tomorrow

My dad died just three weeks before his 60th birthday, unexpectedly. With his sudden death some family members were never able to address certain issues and it made the loss a lot more difficult. Wisdom teaches us to keep relationships positive and current with no unfinished business, as we are not guaranteed tomorrow, only today.

Think about this truth: "Ninety percent for today and ten percent for the future." As I have grown in my personal faith and professional career, the ten percent for God and ninety percent for us is a good rule for our finances and our time. We cannot do anything about our past and are not guaranteed tomorrow, so all we have for sure is today. My encouragement is to invest in relationships today; invest that money in people and experiences today; use the time today for the important things as it will be gone at some point and you are unable to get it back.

The goal of the bedrock truth of applying ninety percent today and ten percent for tomorrow is often evidenced in not having regrets or at least minimizing any regrets you may have.

Have you experienced a sudden death of a loved one? Have you found yourself within a life event that shook you to your core and forced you into a journey you were not planning, or prevented you from doing something that was on your bucket list, if you had one?

One of the most important areas to focus on in life is relationships. The goal needs to be, "Keep relationships positive and current and with no unfinished business, as you are not guaranteed tomorrow, only today." Positive relationships set a foundation for success in all the other areas in your life because it frees up energy and emotion to be all that you can be no matter what you face. It also naturally builds up strong friendships with people who can help you or who you can help in their journey; therefore, the load is not as heavy or carried alone.

Procrastination never works. You've heard of the Procrastinator's Convention? They wanted to plan it but kept putting it off. A procrastinator shelves what he or she can or should do today and projects toward doing it tomorrow. Under the pure definition, when the procrastinator wakes up the next day, tomorrow becomes today and the cycle of doing what could be done today repeats itself tomorrow. Have you ever felt as though you have been caught in this trap and time slips away from you and items seem to never get done or the important issues resolved?

Have you seen elements of procrastination crop up in your finances? "I cannot afford to give to the church or that organization or cause today, but I will do it someday." "We will do that family vacation next year when there is more time and money." I am reminded of a story where a rich man put in his will that he wanted to take all his gold that he had acquired during his lifetime up to heaven when he died. At his funeral his casket was surrounded with gold bricks, carefully laid around his body. When he got up to heaven, everyone celebrated his arrival but they were curious why he brought paving stones along with him!

What is valuable here is not valuable in heaven, so we should use what we have here wisely while on earth. Put another way, our time on earth is a boot camp to build the character we will take to heaven and that is all we will bring along with us. My counsel: use this earthly time wisely to build the character you want for an eternity!

Another part of this equation focuses on how we plan for and how we approach the future. Perhaps you are blessed and you live a long life and age gracefully or maybe not so gracefully. At some point you may have to ask yourself if you properly planned for your needs in your future. You may have to ask, "Are my relationships strong and fulfilling? Do I have enough money to retire and live on?" Again, the key to the ninety percent today and the ten percent tomorrow maxim is not to have regrets but it's to appropriately meet current and future needs by planning and taking appropriate action.

The future is difficult if not impossible to predict, so how can we put ourselves into a position of having no or few regrets in something we have so little knowledge? One great resource is tapping into people that represent good role models, those who have already gone through the journey before you. Ask these role models questions about their journey. Even though their journeys may be very different than yours, you can still learn the bedrock truths. As we age, perspective is gained and varied experiences often become similar. Acquiring advice and counsel from those who are providing good examples is valuable in putting the pieces together for an effective plan in your life.

We cannot predict the future (no one can with certainty), but we can harness the knowledge of people who are going through or have already gone through the life stage or stages for which you may be planning.

For my wife and me, we tapped into our parents and older friends a lot, especially in child rearing. Raising children can be scary, but if you harness the knowledge and wisdom of someone who is in a stage ahead of you, that knowledge gained can make your journey much more enjoyable and help build skills that affect other aspects of your life.

In dealing with the loss of a loved one, how comforting it was to have friends who had been through this kind of loss years earlier, and in them I could see hope that life will continue to be good. They exemplified what I needed in real life.

The investments we made in our church and the people in our community over the twenty years we lived in California brought much joy to me and my family. I could never have imagined the amount of support and love that would come to us in our time of need when my wife was diagnosed with Stage 4 colon cancer and she spent eighteen months battling with it.

Because we had invested our time, money, and emotion in people, relationships, and good causes over the years, it was an opportunity for them to invest in us in our time of need!

We have a choice in who we choose as friends, but we don't have a choice in who we have as our family. To build that relationship with family, it may and often does require us to get into their worlds. I was very fortunate that both my boys played football and it was a family endeavor. I coached youth football, announced games, and was a member of the youth football board. We not only invested in our children in this sport, but in the children of our community at the same time. Because it was an interest of mine, it was easy to get involved and allocate my time, money, and emotion.

But football was not the entire makeup of our children. Our older son wrestled as a second sport and loved comic books and superhero movies. Our younger son loved music and was a drummer for a band in high school. He also loved the outdoors and got involved in Boy Scouts and eventually became an Eagle Scout. I chose to get involved in things that, at first, I had little or no knowledge of.

For my older son I went to the wrestling tournaments to support him, though I had scarce knowledge of the sport to help him on techniques or preparation for different opponents. So, I brought my nice digital single-lens reflex (SLR) camera and got down at mat side and took pictures. I was able to capture priceless moments for not only my son but for other families as well, and emailed pictures to them throughout the season. I watched superhero movies with him and let my son talk about the different characters and story lines and little things within the story line that most people don't know about.

For my younger son we opened our home to the band for practice, and my wife would always make sure they had something to eat and drink as the practices sometimes were long. Thank goodness they played 1970s and 1980s rock that my wife and I grew up with! We got to know the other band members and their families. They performed at various school performances over the years and we got to enjoy the progress they made along the way. Although the Boy Scouts was a group in which I did not have a lot of time to invest, fortunately there were other adults investing in the program. But I did go as an adult chaperone on camping trips, hikes, and fishing trips, and these memories are priceless. The point? Get involved whether familiarity is present or not.

For my wife, I am sure that where I was most comfortable, she was not. As it was so well written in her memorial, "Still being the 'only girl' in the family, Nancy knew the importance of the winning touchdown or the elusive takedown in her sons' lives, cheering them on with high enthusiasm." It is important if not vital to get into their worlds which may force you to get out of yours, but the paybacks are worth it!

Think about what makes up positive relationships. I've listed some indicators, below. You may not have the opportunities to demonstrate these qualities in a short time period, but over time, life events will or may allow you to demonstrate these qualities and I encourage you to try.

One of the first evidences of a positive relationship between you and someone else is when that person will drop anything for you when you have that challenging time or crisis in your life. Isn't it true that these challenging times tend to come at the most inconvenient time for you and your friends? When a person drops or postpones their activities to help you in a time of need that is evidence of a strong and positive relationship.

In all relationships there can be conflict, especially when something is done or said that could offend. When conflicts come your way, directly address the issues with the person involved instead of talking to another person about them. Willfully avoiding the "grapevine" discussion and the "behind-the-back discourse" are other evidences of a positive relationship.

Every person has needs and they change with time and life's events. A healthy relationship includes a balance of give and take. If one person takes constantly, and does not give, it indicates an unhealthy or struggling relationship. A healthy relationship gives and takes over time, meeting the needs of all involved. Perhaps one of the greatest hallmarks in this is that balance is present no matter life's circumstances.

When you can talk about controversial topics with others and you don't necessarily share the same views but you continue to respect the other persons for their views and vice versa, this too, is a telltale sign of strong and healthy relationships. I will share in more detail the value of diverse perspectives in Chapter 7, The Power of Diversity. It is wonderful when a relationship values a different perspective on issues and even where differences of opinion occur, respect is present and people are honored for who they are.

A positive relationship would never require anyone to compromise their values. When an uncomfortable situation arises, being free and confident to speak up and say "no" is important as is the recognition that your "no" will be respected. If the other person wants to pressure you to perform an action that is contrary to your values, watch out! This is a red flag and is an indicator of a negative relationship. A true friend will not want to put another friend in a compromised position.

If a relationship is positive in key areas it will likely be positive in most areas. Relationships should not be hard, but they do require work to keep them healthy. Here's the key: be the friend to others that you want others to be to you!

Think for a moment about your family members or others who are important to you. Are there areas you should get involved in today for the good of them and you? Are there causes or organizations that are important to you because of a greater cause? These investments pay off well, so don't procrastinate. Start your involvement today!

> Ten percent for God and ninety percent for us
> is a good rule for our finances and our time.

Review and Respond

1. Into what great causes do you invest your time and energy?

   _____

   _____

   _____

   _____

   _____

2. What do you regret? Why?

   _____

   _____

   _____

   _____

   _____

   _____

3. How do you know when relationships are strong? How can you make them stronger, and what results do you think you could achieve when strong relationships are present?

_____

_____

_____

_____

_____

_____

4. How has procrastination impacted your life?

_____

_____

_____

_____

_____

_____

5. What important changes would you like to make within yourself to help you enjoy your future with your family and friends?

_____

_____

_____

_____

_____

_____

6. Why is getting involved in areas that may not be in your comfort zone sometimes a very good course of action?

_____

_____

_____

_____

_____

_____

Bedrock Truth #6

Big Windshield Looking Forward, Small Mirror Looking Back

Approach life from the viewpoint of the driver's seat: with a "big windshield looking forward and a small rearview mirror looking back." It is more important to continue to look forward and navigate effectively through life than to constantly look back in the review mirror. We should glance at it periodically to gain perspective or lessons we can apply to our journey, but our primary focus is ahead.

There is a funny play on words that people have used in place of "getting hysterical"; it is, "getting historical!" Have you ever done it or seen someone get historical? Man, they can bring up so much stuff from the past and go on and on about what happened in the past. Did continually recounting all of the past do any good to address any issue at hand?

In football we had a line we lived by after someone made a bad play and was distracted with the results of that play.

Because we had only twenty-five seconds before the next play would begin, the question we would ask is, "What is the most important play?" "It's the *next* play, so you'd better get your head back in the game!" For someone playing music, it is even more critical to get back on note as quickly as you can if one should be missed. Many activities are continuous and require a quick recovery. It's just life.

It is amazing how much energy we can spend on something we can do nothing to change. Does that mean we don't look back and reflect and learn? Absolutely not! But reflection needs to be brief so that we can get back to the issues at hand.

How we use the windshield in a car and the review mirror makes up a great example on how we should look at life. The windshield represents our journey: where we are going; and the rearview mirror represents looking back to where we have been. Could you imagine if the mirror and windshield sizes were reversed, where the mirror was much larger looking back than the windshield that allows us to look forward?

Have you ever managed your life like this or seen someone else do it? Talk about a scary ride that I don't want to be on!

Life is a journey and, like a road, is not always straight. It can have hazards to avoid and many points of interest to take in and enjoy. There may be turns that need to be made or detours along the way. If we stay focused on the rearview mirror, curves will be missed and we will drive off the road. Hazards would come our way and we would not be able to avoid them, which in turn could ruin our day or get us hurt.

Conversely, how many enjoyable moments would be missed because we would observe them only as we passed? We would see the points of interest fade away as we continued down a directionless path.

When is it appropriate to look back? As I write this chapter, I am in San Diego, California. I visited Pacific Beach where our family spent a couple great vacations when our children were young. I felt so much enjoyment from looking back through the rearview mirror and reminiscing about the good times we had on those vacations!

Looking through the rearview mirror can help us evaluate what has worked and what has not worked for us, empowering us to better navigate what is in front of us. Great lessons can be learned in these moments. Reflect back on advice you received or a life event that gave meaning or context to the present events in your life. What did you learn that helps you today?

The key is not to keep our singular focus on what was because then we will miss what is in front of us and not be able to navigate as well as we should. Obviously, our enjoyment on that part of our journey would be negatively affected.

If you want to be an effective leader, adhering to this bedrock truth of focusing on the big windshield looking forward and not the small rearview mirror looking back is powerful. When I was a young engineer, just out of college, my first manager did a wonderful job of leading like this. Confidence was built within me because he focused mostly on current and future successes and only looked back to celebrate or learn key truths relevant to current issues at hand. When people feel good and are confident, the best is brought out in them, empowering them to perform at their highest levels possible.

I would argue that most contemporary performance management processes hone in on what you haven't done versus the great things that you have accomplished. The tendency is to focus in the past versus looking forward, shining a light on how to make you even more effective by utilizing your strengths and developing your potential in areas that will enhance your performance. Instead, common performance evaluation processes concentrate on assigning a score that ranks achievement based on a standard where 80% to 85% of employees simply "just meet expectations." Who wants to be a part of a group that *just* meets expectations?

Looking forward and improving often requires investing in innovation, learning from the past, but not being stuck in it. A simple definition of innovation is this one by Jamie Notter: "Innovation is change that unlocks new value." To unlock this new value, we need to keep our focus through the windshield so we can identify the changes needed and the new value our actions will bring. Is there anyone who would not want to bring new value to their life or to their occupation?

So, let me ask you these questions about your current journey:
1. Where are you going?
2. Who are you leading?
3. How much do you want to focus on what's current and what is in front of you versus staying focused on the past?

The answers to these very important questions will drastically affect how you navigate your journey and how you will lead those who accompany you. You can do nothing about the past, you are not guaranteed tomorrow, you only have the present. Make the most of the present and your enjoyment will naturally increase. That attitudinal change will spill over into so many other aspects of your life!

> Approach life from the viewpoint of the driver's seat:
> with a "big windshield looking forward
> and a small rearview mirror looking back."

Review and Respond

1. Where do you focus most, on your past or present? Why?

_____

_____

_____

_____

_____

2. What have you learned from your past that helps you create and live in your present?

_____

_____

_____

_____

_____

_____

3. How committed are you to driving improvement in yourself or as part of a team when you become aware of the need to make positive changes, personally and professionally?

_____

_____

_____

_____

_____

_____

_____

4. Why is innovation often the key to unlock future potential?

_____

_____

_____

_____

_____

_____

5. Learning from the past prepares us for today. This education is vital to success. So why is the temptation so strong for some to "dwell" in the past instead of using what's been learned to innovate for today and tomorrow?

_____

_____

_____

_____

_____

_____

6. How do we shift our focus from yesterday to where we are going today? What are your specific action steps?

_____

_____

_____

_____

_____

_____

Bedrock Truth #7

The Power of Diversity

I love to use football as an analogy for teamwork. I was a linebacker and we all know that linebackers are good looking, athletic, and smart. But how good would a team be with 53 linebackers? You need offensive linemen, defensive linemen, and they are different from one another. Quarterbacks, running backs, receivers, defensive backs, and yes, even kickers who may not have real pads or helmets — but when you need that extra point, field goal, or well-placed punt, they are critical to team success. "Power of diversity of skills and thought" is the theme here and it applies to any team who is looking for high performance. "If two people think alike, one of them is not needed."

Over my life and especially during my mid-career, my employer had our leadership team do numerous teambuilding exercises. One specific exercise that stands out is a scenario where you are stranded in the cold and it is snowing heavily. There will be no cars coming by and you need to survive the night out in the elements. There are thirteen items in the car and you are to prioritize in order what items you thought were best suited in your effort to survive the situation. Some of the items were a cigarette lighter, compass, map, candy bar, rearview mirror, and the list went on. A scoring system was based on how close you prioritized your list to the perfect prioritized survivalist list. I am not a survivalist, but I am competitive and wanted to get a high enough score to survive! Out of a group of about twenty participants, only about two or three achieved a high enough score to survive!

The next step was to break up into groups of about four each and do the exercise again. This time everyone reached the score to survive and the total scores were higher than the individual scores. Working together works!

Perhaps you've heard this joke before: There is a head-on car accident and the four eyewitnesses were a minister, doctor, mechanic, and a lawyer. The minister prays for all the people involved in the accident. The doctor focuses his attention on the severity of the injuries of the people involved in the accident. The mechanic is evaluating the damage to the car and how significant it is and is concerned about getting a tow truck to get the cars removed from the busy road. The lawyer is handing out business cards and collecting evidence and eye witnesses for a law suit! This story represents how each person with a different background looked at the same event with a different perspective and focused on specific information important only to them.

In 33 years of my professional life, I still have not found that one person who had all the information, experience, and skills to come up with the best solution by themselves. My experience is that to come up with the best solution, perspectives need to come from a range of three to seven people, with five being a good number to cover most common situations. You want diverse team members with varying perspectives to cover the areas that are most important.

For example, in manufacturing we would have someone from operations who runs the equipment, someone representing maintenance that installs and maintains it, someone from quality and/or safety to ensure these aspects are addressed, and someone from engineering who will be responsible for managing the project and considering all the technological challenges. Depending on the type of project, there may be a need from research/marketing/sales if you are in product development. Some of the perspectives may overlap, but it is important to ensure that the selected team members cover different aspects of the issue to be addressed as the figure below shows.

> "If two people think alike, one of them is not needed."

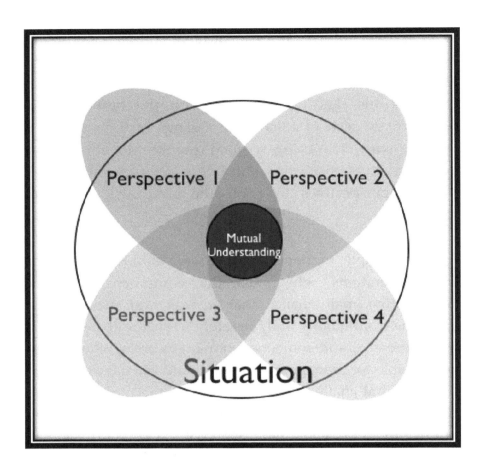

Just imagine how the project would have been addressed if the teams were composed *only* of engineers, *only* of operations personnel, or *only* of maintenance personnel. The final solution would be much more one-dimensional and most likely not meet the needs of the others not represented. These people all may be very highly qualified in their respective skill sets, but it wouldn't take too long to see that far more diverse viewpoints are required to come up with the most effective solutions. Remember, if two of people think alike, one of them is not needed!

Another important point is that there are no stupid or dumb questions or points of view. Even though most may not even be considered, the process may stimulate creative and innovative thinking and become a catalyst for other conversation or ideas that float to the top as the most effective solution.

I see society taking diversity of thought out of our workforce, especially in how our high schools try to prep all students to go to college. Most high schools have either no vocational training or the program has been significantly reduced in size and there are fewer choices of programs. As parents, are we doing the same?

When I look at just the industries I have worked in, there are a diverse set of skills needed and not all of them come from having college degrees. For example: instrument/electrical technicians, mechanics, refrigeration technicians, and operators for manufacturing equipment, just to name a few. They all pay well and offer great career paths for people that have that aptitude.

I would challenge society to not only focus on whether or not someone has a degree; rather, the excellence of function they provide and the contribution to the team are the attributes we should value and recognize. The next time a nurse, car mechanic, food service employee, or plumber give you excellent service, recognize them for it by sharing how their excellence in function/service has impacted your life.

The next time you have a challenging situation in your personal life or at work, look for a diverse group of perspectives you can tap into. Remember, if they all think like you, you may use them only if you want to be told what you want to hear or confirm whatever you have decided anyway.

But if you want to consider many aspects of the situation to come up with the best course of action with given information, get outside your box of comfort and tap into the diversity of the people around you. There is an old saying: "Measure twice, cut once." Another: "It is cheaper to change the design on paper than in the field."

In managing complex and/or important situations, "Plan wisely before moving forward." The best plan often requires acquiring and evaluating the opinion, action, and competence of more than one qualified individual.

Review and Respond

1. A secure person values the input of experts. If that is true, what does that truth say about an insecure person?

_____

_____

_____

_____

_____

2. How much do you value the power of diversity of skills and thought in your business and experience?

_____

_____

_____

_____

_____

_____

3. What examples can you recall of employing varying
    opinions in a project that led to success?

    _____

    _____

    _____

    _____

    _____

    _____

    _____

4. What kinds of attitudinal and action support should
    team members willingly give each other when
    seeking solutions from a wide range of perspectives?

    _____

    _____

    _____

    _____

    _____

    _____

    _____

Bedrock Truth #8

Conflict Is Not Bad;
Only Unresolved Conflict Is Bad

I have tried to pass this truth down to my boys as I have found this topic to be so true in my life. "Conflict is not bad; only unresolved conflict is bad." It is in the process of resolving the conflict that the most effective solutions emerge. This process allows for a joint resolution that provides a better solution for all. It also helps to build strong relationship bonds because of the trust it builds from resolving the conflict.

I was fortunate to have a positive experience at an early age in dealing with conflict and how to fix it. I was a senior in high school and like most kids in a small school, I played multiple sports where one or two were not your primary sport. For me, basketball was not my primary sport as I was about 6'1", almost 200 pounds and played center. I competed against players that were taller than me and could jump higher. I had to play smart and physical.

My girlfriend's dad, later my father-in-law, would remind me quite often what a waste it was that I played basketball and that I would have made a great 189-pound wrestler! My job was simple: play tough defense, set picks on offense, and box out for rebounds. So I thought.

It was midseason and I would start the games but I saw my playing time get less and less in the third and fourth quarters. I can still remember the game where I started but played little in the third and not at all in the fourth. I was not a happy camper to say the least. I showered and got dressed and went up to Coach and said, "I need to talk to you, Coach." Coach told me to get on the bus and he would call me up once we were on the road.

I sat patiently waiting to be called up and my emotions started to ease up some. I finally got the notice to come up. I told the coach, "You always tell me what a good job I do but I haven't been playing as much in the second half of games lately. Tonight, I didn't even play in the fourth quarter!" Coach went on to say that he needed a scoring threat out on the floor and I wasn't a scoring threat. I quickly shot back, "But you never asked me to score points and I thought it was best to pass the ball out." Coach continued to talk about the need for me to score from the close position I normally was in, and suggested some moves to work on.

I did work on the moves in practice and especially shooting with my left hand when I was on the left side of the basket so that my shot was farther away from the defender. As I made the changes to my game, I started scoring points and the team defended me more closely. What this allowed was that when I was guarded really tight, I could pass the ball out and my teammates had closer, more open shots. The result was our team performed better!

At the end of the regular season, we went into the district basketball tournament without high expectations as we were an undersized team and were not great shooters. Who would have guessed that we would win the district tournament and would advance on to the regional tournament? Our lack of size and talent got us eliminated early, but I still remember the locker room conversation after my last high school basketball game. Coach came up to me and said, "Bud, you have exceeded my expectations this year." That is about all I remember of the next couple of minutes as he talked about my contributions to the team.

What I took away from this event is this: I had a valid issue in that I wanted to play more, especially late in the games. The coach had a valid issue in that he wanted to do what was best for the team. With both of us willing to work together to address the issue of my playing time, the benefits expanded to the entire team.

Another key takeaway is this: "Take the initiative." If I would have waited for the coach to come to me, I don't know if the issue would have ever been brought up or addressed. By taking the initiative, I ensured it got addressed.

Because I treated the coach with respect, he, in return, showed respect back to me. This set up an environment for success in dealing with the issue.

It took action from both of us to turn this situation positive; the coach had to give me constructive feedback, and I had to take action on it. If I hadn't taken action, the frustration would have remained and the results would have been far less satisfying and educational.

How valuable is patience in conflict resolution? It was probably in my best interest that the coach made me wait before we discussed the issue because it allowed my emotions to settle down. When you or the person you want to resolve conflict with is emotionally charged, it often is best to wait for a better moment to deal with the issue so emotions won't get in the way.

I can only imagine how differently things would have ended up had I gotten bitter and talked negatively about Coach. It probably would have affected how I acted toward him and how I played. The biggest effect could have been that the team would not have performed as well late in the season and the team may not have experienced the cutting down of the nets after we won the District Championship.

Instead, the coach and I gained mutual respect for each other and ended the season on a positive note. This successful resolution to a potentially negative issue gave me the confidence to deal with conflict effectively throughout my life and I have benefitted from the strengthened relationships it has developed along my journey.

You may be saying, "I only wish I had conflict that easy to resolve, since most of my issues are much more complicated!" Another example of conflict I had to work much harder to resolve involved a performance issue with a direct report.

This direct report was a peer, just a few years younger than me and, looking back, I didn't identify some of the lack of respect and lack of follow-through issues with other problem areas which needed to be resolved; he was taking no responsibility for his subpar performance issues. We conducted a 360 evaluation* and I gave what I thought was constructive feedback from other work groups, peers, and site leadership. When the process was completed, I asked for his feedback and what he believed he could do to address his performance concerns. What I got was a lot of behavior justification. This person told me that he didn't like the high fives that I would give when I was excited about something and would prefer thumbs up. I also got feedback about how my gregarious personality made him feel uncomfortable.

*https://en.wikipedia.org/wiki/360-degree_feedback

Wanting to contribute to a better work environment for this individual, I tried to be conscientious and meet some of the needs of this employee. As the next performance management cycle came around, little change had occurred even after all the feedback throughout the year. When I reviewed the employee's performance evaluation of himself, he gave himself 4s and 5s and I was evaluating behaviors at 2s and 3s. As you can see, there was a big variance in how we each perceived the same performance, and I was frustrated at what I perceived to be a communication gap, even after I had worked so diligently to improve it.

I went into the employee's office and asked my first question. "Do you feel that your evaluation of your performance accurately represents the performance you had this year?" The employee said yes. The next question I asked was, "Do you feel I have your best interest in mind?" The employee said no. My response back was, "We will do your performance review tomorrow morning with the HR Manager and the Site Manager attending," and walked out. This employee immediately went directly to the HR manager and shared how he didn't have the best year and would work on addressing the issues. It was a total change of heart about his performance by the time we met the next day.

What I learned is that sometimes people don't take responsibility and they justify their feelings and actions because of how they feel about the person they have conflict with, in spite of a 360-process designed to reveal the truth. In this case, I needed to obtain perspectives that the employee valued or at least respected as part of the self-evaluation and allow and encourage the employee to take responsibility for his own performance management based on what other co-workers whom the employee trusted had said.

Had I been more aware of this lack of responsibility and how easily it could be addressed by getting others involved who the employee valued, I would have asked his permission to engage coworkers much earlier. Once I got others involved, it wasn't a message just coming from someone the employee did not respect or was uncomfortable with, resulting in justified inaction or blaming the situation on someone else. The message from others that was consistent with the feedback the employee had received all along moved the person into taking personal responsibility and action toward improving his performance. The working relationships were much better from then on as we both took responsibility to make it better.

Most of the time in difficult situations, it is valuable to get appropriate people who are neutral and not emotionally attached to the conflict being addressed. In my case, HR was that neutral third party, and involving HR is usually an option in a work environment.

Outside of work, it may be more difficult, but you need to identify someone who will be confidential with the information shared and then assure that the other person fully agrees to their involvement before initiating any action. A person held in mutual respect is one who will be confidential and is one who will not be emotionally engaged. These are desired key attributes of a third party.

The goal is to have objective mediators who work together effectively through the issues. This is not a process to get numbers on your side or to gang up on employees; rather, this is a process involving people with maturity and discernment to help resolve conflict. The goal always has to be a win/win!

> It is in the process of resolving conflict that the most effective solutions emerge.

Review and Respond

1. What are your preferred methods of dealing with conflict? How well do they work?

   _____

   _____

   _____

   _____

   _____

2. How do you *know* when conflict is actually "resolved"? What are the obvious signs that hurt or severed relationships have been healed and restored?

   _____

   _____

   _____

   _____

   _____

   _____

3. In any process of conflict resolution, at least one person has to take the initiative to begin it. What does, or should, taking initiative look like?

_____

_____

_____

_____

_____

_____

4. We are told that patience is a virtue. Perhaps in few other ways than conflict resolution is this true. Agree or disagree? Why?

_____

_____

_____

_____

_____

_____

5. How important is mutual respect when resolving differences and how is it demonstrated?

_____

_____

_____

_____

_____

_____

6. Why is choosing humility necessary to create solutions to end conflict and restore relationships?

_____

_____

_____

_____

_____

_____

_____

Bedrock Truth #9

You Can Reason Only with Reasonable People

You can reason only with reasonable people. I am amazed how so many television talking heads love to debate foreign policy, and with so many conflicts, they think we can negotiate and reason with the enemy. I found out early on the playground and in work that you cannot reason with unreasonable people, and the sooner you find that out the better.

Sometimes it's best to remove yourself from the issue or scene. But if the issue is critical enough, it may require physical action to address it or the present hazard. I have only been in about four fights in my life but numerous times I used my size and strength to address pressing issues. I have also tried to pass this down to my boys because they are big and strong, too. I've often told them that if you use your size and strength for good, it will bring rewards.

Today you also have to be aware that really bad people don't fight fair as they could have knives and guns, and may not care what level of pain they inflict. So, try not to put yourself or others in a compromised position. Again, know when to remove yourself from the situation, because more harm than good can come from getting involved in many negative situations.

When we were teenagers, we often thought that our parents could not be reasoned with—because *they* were unreasonable. When I was seventeen years old, I had a chance to buy a 1965 Mustang Convertible or a 1969 Boss Mustang. My father looked me in the eye and said, "As long as you live in this house, you will never drive a convertible!" What made this statement confusing for me was that when I was fourteen, he signed a loan so I could buy my first street motorcycle! Convertible not okay; motorcycle okay?

Being a compliant child, I went on and bought the 1969 Boss Mustang for $2,900. In the long run it was a better investment and I still don't know exactly why he felt so strongly against convertibles. What I learned was there was a better season to own a convertible. Later in my life when Nancy, my wife, and I were Double Income No Kids, (DINK's as we were called then), we would buy a 1969 GT Mustang Convertible with a 351 4-barrel carburetor and 4-speed transmission!

What is an unreasonable person? My definition is this: an unreasonable person is someone who is not willing to consider anyone else's needs but only their own no matter what message you have or what circumstances are presented. Certainly, they are not considering yours. They are not open to other opinions. Some are that way all the time and some only get there when they are emotionally elevated. At first glance, you may think that my father was only thinking of his own interest about what car he would allow me to buy, but as I look back, living in South Dakota with cold weather, a convertible may not have been the most feasible everyday car. He may also have had issues with the safety of a convertible since I was a teenage driver at the time.

One stereotypical version of an unreasonable person is what we call a bully, and they show up throughout our lives. Even though my two boys were big, strong, smart, and athletic, they were not spared the emotional distress of dealing with bullies. The bullying was verbal in nature and always took place at school on the playground where they could show off to their friends. Many of the bullies were smaller and knew that the school had a no tolerance for physical contact. With verbal bullying it was your word against theirs, and most of the time nothing of consequence happens and this empowers the bully to do it more.

I made it clear to my boys that they were not to take physical action unless they were threatened, and we defined threatened as this: if the bully threw the first punch. In that circumstance, you had to go into self-defense mode. But threatened can also be defined as when you tell the other person to stay away or their presence will or could be considered a threatening act. If they cross that line, then it is okay to take action.

I still remember when my oldest son, Grant, was thirteen and in the 8th grade. He was sharing with his mother and I that he felt like a bear in a zoo at school. The bullies are like the visitors to the zoo and they are poking at him through the bars of the cage. If he was to retaliate, the zoo would kill him. He shared this as tears came down his cheeks.

A year later when he was a freshman in high school, he came across a bullying incident. A sophomore, who had played youth football with my son, was being bullied by another sophomore. My son intervened and the bully started trash-talking my son for getting involved. The bully went on his way and the next day caught my son between classes after PE (physical education). Again, the bully verbally taunted my son to get him to throw the first punch. My son did not want a physical altercation and the possible consequences he would receive from the school and at home. Then, out of nowhere, the bully threw two punches to my son's face. Grant was a wrestler, so he grabbed the bully and put him in a submission hold on the grass until a school administrator showed up.

The result was that both of them got suspended from school and extra-curricular activities for a week. The bully had no desire to be in school and wasn't involved in school activities. My son played football and wrestled. He missed the football banquet where he was freshman lineman of the year and two wrestling tournaments. Was that equal punishment?

The good news is that the head football coach brought Grant's award to him in class the following week and from then on, he had no trouble with that kid and any other bullies.

My younger son, Brett, has a similar situation and it developed in his senior year of high school. There was a boy who was a year younger and much smaller and he would make fun of my son in front of a girl he liked. Brett was disappointed mostly in that the friend of the boy was someone Brett had played basketball with for years going back to 8th grade. This classmate would never stand up for Brett or hold his friend accountable. Brett turned the other cheek until one day the bully used the girl's phone to text a very inappropriate message and Brett knew the bully had done it. The crazy thing was the school's video system caught the entire event and the video was used as evidence.

Brett saw the bully across the gym and took a straight line walking very fast across the gym to confront him about the incident. Brett basically told him that he knew he used the girl's cell phone for the inappropriate text and that he needed to stop it and not do it anymore. The bully started trash-talking Brett and took his backpack off to antagonize Brett. That action appeared to be threatening, so Brett threw the first punch and the bully hit the floor. The bully got up and went after Brett again. Brett put him in a headlock and started punching him in the head a few times until he fell to the floor. Brett left the scene and the incident was over in less than 30 seconds.

I got a call at work from a deputy sheriff asking me if I was aware of an incident involving my son at school. I said I was not and he went on to say there was an incident with my son and another boy where they got into a physical confrontation and the deputy sheriff wanted to know if I wanted to press charges. If I did, the boys would be taken to Juvenal Hall until the issue was sorted out. I had to ask again what he was referring to as the furthest thing on my mind was that Brett was in a fight since he had never been in a fight his entire life.

Brett was suspended for a week. There was a lot of emotion in the school about the incident, and the administrators were very disappointed that Brett took the action he did even though they knew the other boy had issues. The craziest thing was that a few weeks later, the boy Brett had experienced the incident with was on crutches and when he approached a door that Brett was standing near, Brett opened the door for him. Brett started a conversation with the boy by asking questions about his knee, because Brett had had the ACL (anterior cruciate ligament) in his knee replaced the year before. The boy shared how he hurt it in basketball and they had a great talk. I think they got over the incident faster than many other people in the school. The rest of the school year there were no more incidents with Brett or other bullies.

The unfortunate part is that my boys wish they would have dealt with the issues earlier by confronting the bullies physically. They tried to get along and they turned the other cheek for years. Once they took action, the issues stopped immediately. The positive thing is that both of them have developed empathy for the outsiders, geeks, and the less fortunate who are typical targets for bullies, and they include them into their circle and stick up for them.

Here is the issue with dealing with difficult people: the consequences for you may be higher than the consequences for the offending person. In all cases physical action can get you in trouble and in today's world you don't know who may have guns and knives, so I don't advocate for most people to resolve a bullying incident with physical response.

A risk also exists of getting assault charges placed against you as most unreasonable people want to make it as difficult on you as possible. An accident where someone hits a corner of a hard object or a punch that has more power than expected can cause severe injury or death. Confrontations with results like these could produce life-long negative consequences for everyone involved. For most of us, our places of work have a zero tolerance for physical contact, and you would be fired on the spot if any physical contact occurred like what I am describing.

At my work I have seen many times where an unreasonable person instigates an issue. If the issue was reported, it would only be an issue with the unreasonable person. Things are often said or done in the state of anger or frustration and that elevates the altercation into an issue for both parties, and then both have to be disciplined.

So how do you respond to unreasonable people? The first thing is to identify who is being unreasonable, and that may be easy to see since most of them display this characteristic on a regular basis. If you can, avoid them! If not, minimize your time and topics if you deal with them one on one. And if necessary, have a witness.

One of the keys to dealing with emergencies is planning and writing out a plan on how to deal with them. During the emergency is _not_ the time to do the planning as we don't do our best planning and thinking in stressful situations. The same type of plan needs to be thought through and chosen ahead of time on dealing with unreasonable people.

Questions to consider could be these:

1. What kind of actions would cause you to remove yourself from the situation?
2. When do you get involved, what kinds of actions require reporting the incidents to an appropriate authority?

The first thing I consider is whether I can have a positive influence on the perpetrators or will they have a larger negative impact on me? If their behavior still allows you to have a positive impact in their life, then develop a plan on how to move forward with this person to produce the most favorable and positive result.

It is one thing when the unreasonable person is someone with whom you work and share occasional time, or someone you cross paths with infrequently. But what if the offending party is someone you work for or with, and having regular, ongoing contact with them is required or frequent? What if it's a next-door neighbor, or how about a family member?!

You need to get alternate perspectives from people who have demonstrated skills in dealing with negative people and confrontational issues. Listening to and learning from fresh perspectives may allow you to come up with a plan that will be the most effective at bringing the most out of the relationship.

I cannot stress this enough: do not engage negative or bullying people when either of you are emotionally elevated!

The condition of our heart is the most critical in dealing with unreasonable people, since our heart, or our core, controls our actions. We need to control our responses effectively because we cannot control how other people act or respond. Further, part of our planning process is to evaluate our heart to ensure it is in alignment toward effective resolution should the conditions present themselves. The goal should always be to improve the relationship and make it a win/win.

The key is that both parties are open to work within this supportive environment. Be patient; the environment may not be healthy today but the unreasonable person may show a change of heart at a later time. The best testimony and example you can have is the willingness to move forward when the other party has a change of heart and forgive them whether or not their heart attitude changes. Sometimes you have to be happy and celebrate the small improvements when complete resolution is not in the cards.

Have you ever dealt with an unreasonable person, where it seems that there was no path to find middle ground for a resolution? What were the emotions and feelings like in dealing with that person in a negative circumstance? One of the most challenging things is to manage unreasonable people effectively in difficult situations. And if done properly, it can lay a foundation to make tough relationships better and increase the enjoyment on the part of your journey that has difficult people in it.

> The best testimony and example you can have
> is the willingness to move forward when the other party
> has a change of heart and forgive them whether or not
> their heart attitude changes.

Review and Respond

1. Recognizing injustice and bullying is the first step toward planning how to confront the issues appropriately. What telltale signs of bullying have you witnessed and how have you addressed them?

_____

_____

_____

_____

_____

2. Do you believe it is possible to make peace with everyone? Why or why not?

_____

_____

_____

_____

_____

3. What part do humility and forgiveness play in the resolution of personal or professional conduct, and when should these attributes be offered and received?

_____

_____

_____

_____

_____

_____

_____

4. How do you handle situation where consequences are unfairly and unjustly applied?

_____

_____

_____

_____

_____

_____

5. If possible, avoid negative, bullying, pushy, intimidating, and threatening people. If you cannot avoid them, what is your plan to confront them and the issues they create that involve you?

_____

_____

_____

_____

_____

6. Have you ever experienced a tough relationship that was improved through mutual understanding and forgiveness? What were the hallmarks of this restitution and how did you feel when a relationship was created or restored?

_____

_____

_____

_____

_____

_____

Bedrock Truth #10

All Things Work Together for Good to Those Who Love God

I think we have all heard the saying, "The only absolutes in life are death and taxes." Benjamin Franklin was right on the mark when he said it. While we may agree with his statement, I also think there is another absolute. It is this: trials and difficult times come into everyone's life.

The severity, the timing, and the specifics may all be different, but there are challenges for everyone to face. In fact, knowing this truth can help us prepare.

Please think about people you admire. Why do you admire them? Is it because of how they deal with the good times, or how well they handle the tough times in the trials and challenges of life, or both? I have been so fortunate to have great role models, and one common theme with all of them is that they dealt with life issues well, the good and the bad. This choice maximized the joy in their journeys, and that choice has allowed me to maximize the joy in my journey as well.

A recent challenge in my life was when my high school sweetheart and wife of twenty-six years, was diagnosed with Stage 4 Colon Cancer in December of 2013. It blindsided us really badly as Nancy was only 49 years old, with no family history of colon cancer in her family, and no risk factors.

Removal of the tumor in the colon required surgery and this proved to be the easy part of the journey that was to follow. The cancer had metastasized throughout the entire liver. The only reason my wife even went to the doctor was because she had a pain in her side that would not go away. Surgery to remove the tumors in the liver was not an option, so managing the cancer was the road ahead for us.

To add to our stress, my job had been eliminated about three months before and I was still looking for work. I was insured to the end of the year and then it was COBRA insurance at $1,700 per month. The silver lining in this situation was that being unemployed allowed me to go to all the doctor appointments and chemo treatments with Nancy and be a valuable second set of ears and mind. It is amazing how much a person can miss when your current reality is so clouded with the challenges ahead and with all the new terms you get to learn dealing with cancer for the first time.

The process of getting care, interfacing with the medical professionals, and our church/community support was unbelievable. As scared as we were, there was reassurance all around us, encouraging us to fight the battle against cancer.

Nancy and I prioritized our list of desires and actions, to ensure that the energy she did have was used living life as well as we could. Meals were brought in, firewood brought to the house, and my big rounds split by a couple of guys at the church. Friends stopped by and loved on us. My mother has reminded me about what she calls The Three-Day Rule, "Fish and company have one thing in common: they start to stink after three days." Well, she came and stayed for eight days—and no stink!

A life memory during this time was when I told my mother how this lady had brought a chicken and dumpling meal and that it had reminded me of the homemade chicken and noodles she made when I was young. I asked her if she could make this meal for us. My mother agreed but insisted we needed to obtain a farm chicken to get the best flavor since they are so much better than any store-bought chicken. Brett, my younger son, went to school and found a classmate who raised chickens and we bought one. Brett brought it home in a dog carrier where it stayed until the next morning. My mother would have nothing to do with chopping the head off of the chicken, so Brett and I did that. The rest of the processing of the chicken and making the homemade noodles was a team effort of my mother and my son. What a great time of sharing this became and it will be remembered for a lifetime.

But the challenges did not end. Finding work within an hour of where we had built our forever home on ten acres with a view of the Sierra Mountains, was not coming together. So, I started looking outside the hour drive and ended up getting a great offer with a company that would require us to move to the Portland, Oregon area. After all we had been going through and having enjoyed and nourished the relationships of the church family and community we had built up after twenty years of experiencing life together, now we had to move!

We moved to the State of Washington in August of 2014, and key details of the move just started lining up. We bought a house with a great view of the Columbia River and Mt. Hood. Our neighbors were great. We had 30 different friends and relatives that visited us over the next year. This was a new world for Nancy and me to explore together, as well as with family and friends.

Waking up and having breakfast and drinking coffee in the morning together is much different than someone just stopping by. We got up in the morning and saw each other with bed head and in pajamas. We cooked together in the kitchen and were focused just on the current moment. We planned activities and points of interest that we wanted to visit together. Our relationships were growing and we added many great memories in that year with so many people.

My sister, Kristy, was dealing with Stage 3 breast cancer at the end of 2013 and was living in Austin, Texas. Kristy asked if she could live with us for a year while she dealt with her own cancer challenge. What a blessing her moving in with us turned out to be, as early on when Kristy was down, Nancy was up. When Nancy was down, Kristy was up.

As the year progressed, Kristy's health improved and Nancy's declined. Kristy was a huge blessing in dealing with the pain medications, doing night duty, while I did day duty up until the time when Nancy was hospitalized three times in the last month of her life. She needed the hospitalization to deal with the pain as the cancer took over her body.

Our sons, Grant and Brett, drove from California to visit her in the hospital, and important feelings between a mom and her boys were shared. Nancy got to express how proud she was of them and told them she was glad they were happy. The boys got to share how thankful they were for her being their mom, and to remember key moments that meant so much to them. We even got Nancy in a wheel chair and brought her out to the parking garage so she could see, for the first time, Brett's dog, Loggy, our first grand puppy!

Nancy was a stay-at-home mom and we both began to realize that some of the goals she wasn't going to achieve were being present at her boys' weddings and holding her grandchildren. The best she could do now was to reinforce how proud she was of them and how much she loved them.

Fifty percent of her memorial video was composed of the pictures of the last eighteen months of her life where she lived life well! Some of the more memorable moments: we traveled to Menlo College football games to watch Grant play. We traveled throughout Oregon and Washington with friends and family, experiencing nature and numerous points of interest. Both my mother and sister Gina would play Scrabble with Nancy with such competitive spirit (okay—mostly demonstrated by Nancy!). Nancy decorated our new home so well and hosted a great Christmas dinner, utilizing her mother's Fostoria glassware* for her last Christmas, even though we thought she would have many more to celebrate. Friends came up for New Year's Eve and we toasted to a new year at midnight as we watched fireworks from our deck. There was much laughter and experiencing life with over 30 friends and family members during our first year in our new home in Washington.
*https://en.wikipedia.org/wiki/Fostoria_Glass_Company

As much as we did not want to go down the road with cancer, many positive events occurred during that time with our personal growth, spiritual growth, deeper friendships, and sharing life with people in an entirely different way. This interchange bore testimony, and was an affirmation, to this truth found in Romans 8:28. Quoted here:

[28]And we know that in all things God works for the good of those who love him, who have been called according to his purpose.

When a challenge or tough time comes our way, we all have a choice as to how we will deal with difficult circumstances. The next time a challenge shows up in your life, why not embrace it and become the person you admire? Here's what I recommend: grow your relationship with God, family, and other important people in your life. Evaluate your life and prioritize your desires and actions so the important things are done first and the lower value things are the ones that get knocked down the list and perhaps not done at all.

Live life, so there are no regrets! Choose to be the role model that not only brings joy to your journey, but to the journey of others! In the difficult times, what do you see in yourself? What do others see? What behaviors would you like to change to make living your life's journey an enjoyable one no matter whether you are experiencing the good, or the bad?

I am convinced that God did not give Nancy cancer. I believe that pain and suffering in this world come from The Fall with Adam and Eve. God allowed the cancer, and with His guidance and strength, we dealt with it. Nancy did at times deal with fear and anger because of life changes after diagnosis. God's strength allowed joy to overpower the fear and anger during this very difficult time. When the end was obviously near, Nancy was totally at peace and only because of her faith in God.

Sickness is present in our world. There are bad people doing bad things to good people. There is severe weather that causes harm to people and property.

In these trying times God gives us the strength and hope to best deal with negative issues and genuinely portray our best testimony to ourselves and to others of God's love and provision. I cannot imagine how people deal with difficult life issues without the love and guidance of God.

Without Him, we would have never been able to cope. While we still had pain as we walked the cancer road and although we lost Nancy, we had hope, and we have assurance that God is there to guide and comfort us. There is no better assurance.

When a challenge or tough time comes our way, we all have a choice as to how we will deal with difficult circumstances. The next time a challenge shows up in your life, why not embrace it and become the person you admire?

Review and Respond

1. Pain and pleasure may often coexist in the same set of circumstances. How has this been true in your life?

_____

_____

_____

_____

2. Who are your role models? How often have you thanked them if you know them personally? What examples of their behaviors do you want to see alive in your experiences?

_____

_____

_____

_____

_____

_____

3. When you are going through difficult times, how important is the support of people who genuinely care about you? What are the hallmarks of their involvement?

_____

_____

_____

_____

_____

_____

4. When it seems like all things are *not* working together for good, do you believe circumstances have to change or should you change?

_____

_____

_____

_____

_____

5. How important is faith in God when the tough times come? What is your personal faith journey and how does it help you?

_____

_____

_____

_____

_____

_____

6. The ways we deal with challenge provide illustrations, good or bad, or both, to others. What behavioral changes would you like to make to become a better role model to others who observe how you handle the tough times?

_____

_____

_____

_____

_____

_____

The Enduring Foundation for Change

Ten to One Relationships

Discipline without a relationship leads to rebellion. People quit managers, not companies. People would give up all kinds of money to have a positive work environment. People don't care how much you know until they know how much you care — I am sure you've heard that before. Those are rock solid truths.

From a great book I read long ago, *Leadership Is — How to Build Your Legacy,* "Relationship precedes and gives definition to function". Knowing and implementing **The Ten Bedrock Truths** is *all* about relationships!

Relationships are the foundation to motivate action that allows every Bedrock Truth to work in anyone's life.

I am a gearhead, so the Ten to One phrase is a play on words to represent this: all of **The Ten Bedrock Truths** are dependent on positive healthy relationships. Without them, sustainable change in behaviors is unlikely if not impossible.

Jesus is quoted in **Mathew 22:37-40**:

> [37] Jesus replied: "'Love the Lord your God with all your heart and with all your soul and with all your mind.' [38] This is the first and greatest commandment. [39] And the second is like it: 'Love your neighbor as yourself.' [40] All the Law and the Prophets hang on these two commandments."

What this means: if you love God with all your heart and soul and you love your neighbor as you love yourself, the natural outcome is that you *won't want* to lie, steal, kill, have inappropriate relationships, and you *will want* to honor your mother and father and other commandments. These two greatest commandments are all about instituting, growing, and living within positive relationships.

Being a parent and a manager, I have personally witnessed this truth: without a relationship, if you try to discipline or set rules, the relationship vacuum leads to rebellion or inaction.

The term, "relationship" has many definitions. In *Leadership Is – How to Build Your Legacy*, the meaning consists of the choice, or personal decision I make about your success. If I regard you highly, my behavior will illustrate that I have an interest in your success, and my actions will prove it.

What this means is this: depending on whether you hold another person in high or low regard, or behave positively or negatively towards someone else, demonstrates that the choice is yours and yours alone to endeavor to enter into either a positive or negative relationship with anyone.

In 2004 Nancy and I built our forever home, and what an experience it was. One thing that stands out is the difference between rough framing carpentry and finish carpentry on the inside of the house. When the house is being framed, tape measures are used to quickly measure lengths, and pencils roughly mark the lengths. Then with a circular saw the carpenters get close and make the cut. If it is not perfect, the cut will be covered up with exterior sheeting plus siding, and errors in cuts on the inside will be covered with sheetrock.

On the other hand, when the hardwood stairs and handrails were being assembled, much more care was taken as everything would be exposed, and the materials cost about ten times as much. Better saws and blades were used, much more care was exercised in measuring more precise lengths and angles, and sharper pencils were used in scribing the mark necessary to ensure the work looked good and that minimal material was wasted. It was ten times the work to do the finished carpentry as the rough framing carpentry in building a house. When it is important and visible, it is worth the effort upfront to not make mistakes that are timely and costly to fix. This is the same for relationships.

Have you ever heard the old saying, "One 'oops' wipes away a lot of 'attaboys'"? Relationships live by the same rule. One relational mistake can require many relational fixes. Just for fun I will use the Ten to One rule again: one mistake equals the effort of ten fixes! If you were more aware of the extreme effort to overcome mistakes, would additional consideration be taken on how you react and respond in relationship issues? Another old saying is, "Measure twice and cut once!" This maxim is wise to apply in evaluating responses, especially in stressful situations. Think twice and respond once!

So, let's summarize: first, there is a need to have a positive relationship with God in order to have an enduring standard upon which to build any and all relationships. Once that standard is adhered to, then it follows that we need to work to begin building a relationship with ourselves, yes, ourselves. Only then can we fully engage in creating and living in positive relationships with others.

It is vital to remember the Two Great Commandments (**Matthew 22:37-40**). All precepts flow from them. All positive relationships are dependent on obedience to these two great commands.

³⁷ Jesus replied: "'Love the Lord your God with all your heart and with all your soul and with all your mind.' ³⁸ This is the first and greatest commandment. ³⁹ And the second is like it: 'Love your neighbor as yourself.' ⁴⁰ All the Law and the Prophets hang on these two commandments."

In summary:
1. Love God
2. Love Your Neighbor as Yourself

Remember: these are commands, not recommendations.

Part of living in positive relationships includes accepting God's love and forgiveness personally, and allowing this acceptance to be the model of our forgiveness of others. This acceptance gives us the power to love and forgive: it's belief in action. Obedience in forgiveness is driven and motivated by God's love. It's conditional, too. If we forgive, God forgives us. If we fail to forgive, we remain unforgiven.

> **Mathew 6:14, 15,** quoting Jesus:
> "¹⁴ For if you forgive other people when they sin against you, your heavenly Father will also forgive you. ¹⁵ But if you do not forgive others their sins, your Father will not forgive your sins."

Mathew 5:44, quoting Jesus:
"But I say to you, love your enemies, bless
those who curse you, do good to those who
hate you, and pray for those who spitefully use
you and persecute you…"

The Ten Bedrock Truths point us to God's love; these
work together for the benefit of everyone we contact.

Positive relationships have to be in place to be effective in
implementing any of **The Ten Bedrock Truths**. An
individual needs to have that positive relationship within
that will motivate and inspire action. You cannot give to
others what you do not possess yourself.

Positive relationships have to be in place to be effective in
implementing any of **The Ten Bedrock Truths**.

I developed a simple acronym to illustrate how positive
relationships work. It's all about **HELP**.

H – Offer a Hand Up
E – Experience God's Love personally then
share it with others
L – Love others because God loves you
P – People Need Your Love, just as you receive
God's love

The results are manifest in who you are and all you may do. Building a solid positive foundation within you gives you the strength and courage to better evaluate circumstances and situations and make more informed choices that will result in increasing your enjoyment along your journey, and providing a blessing and inspiration to others. This is a Godly design.

This action will not only bring about positive change in your life, but will become the example to others and could be the catalyst to motivate others into action that will bring positive changes in their lives.

> Another old saying is measure twice and cut once! This is wise to apply to evaluating responses especially in stressful situations. *Think twice and respond once!*

Evaluate responses against the standard of God's love. Only then can we truly **HELP**.

Here's the Bottom Line:
Building a Better You

The Personal Formula for Change

Writing a book was not something I had really ever considered doing, but the opportunity came and I ran with it. I acted on a request of a friend of mine to share ten quotes or life lessons that have impacted my life. As I have reflected on **The Ten Bedrock Truths** in this book, it has brought much joy revisiting key lessons that gave me a foundation on which my wife and I could build a great life.

On our journey we encountered a combination of celebrations, great events, and challenges. Because of the conscience decisions and actions we took, we were able to enjoy many times of success along the way. Courage was built within us to embrace challenges and successes alike. Our choices allowed us to experience enjoyment from the challenges and the good times, too.

I am very thankful for the great people that have been a part of my journey. If relationships were currency, my wife and I would be some of the richest people on earth! Was it because we only encountered good people?

My father-in-law was a realtor and auctioneer and had a story he loved to share. A family is moving into town and drives to a gas station to fill up their car. There is an old man rocking in a rocking chair out in front of the gas station. The husband and wife both said they were moving into town and wanted to know what the people are like here. The old man asked them, "Well, what were the people like where you come from?" The husband said they were great people and they hated to leave. The wife said they had so much fun with their neighbors and friends and that you could not ask for better people. The old man says, "I think you will find the people the same here; they are friendly, and they're people you will enjoy." They left with gas in their tank and smiles on their faces as they drove down the street.

Sometime later another family drives up to the gas station and asks the old man the same question. "We are moving and are new in town and wanted to know what the people are like here." The old man asked them the same question, "Well, what were the people like where you come from?" The man answered, "Oh, they were backstabbers and gossipers. We couldn't wait to get out of there." The old man says, "The people are the same around here."

Are people that much different from one another, or is what we bring out of them one of the elements that makes them different? Does how we interact, and respond to them and the situations we share, make the difference? How do we build relationships? Who do we choose to spend our time with? Do we resolve the conflict or do we add to it?

My wife and I consistently tried to made decisions in the best interest of our family, neighbors, and friends. Many did the same to us in return. If we offended someone or did something that upset them, we took responsibility and tried to make it right. If they were unreasonable, we did what we could to minimize our time with them and focused our energies on healthy relationships that composed a win/win.

The Ten Bedrock Truths are not proprietary in nature, but they are simple, and everyone can benefit from engaging in them. I like "simple," but these truths do take action for them to work. Like the old saying, "Insanity is doing the same thing over and over but expecting different results." If you want different results, you will need to take new actions, and I hope this book has given you some effective actions to consider.

When I coached youth football, one of the sayings I had for the young boys was this: "There are two things you have control over. That is your heart and your hustle. Heart is the willingness and desire to do what is right and learn. Hustle is the effort you put towards something." I would say to the young boys, "If you apply all your heart and hustle, you will compete and contribute to the team's success. If you have talent to go along with your heart and hustle, you will dominate. You don't have control of how much talent you have and how it compares to the talent of other team members, but you do have control over your heart and hustle."

When considering change, three things need to be realistically and honestly evaluated and these are represented in the equation below. First, evaluate the challenges or risks of the current situation. Much of the time we do not effectively do this as we hold to what we are comfortable with and only focus on what we may lose. If we are honest, there are numerous challenges in our current state. Next, realistically and honestly evaluate the benefits of the future state, and in many situations the benefits are not identified due to lack of perspective or effort.

In looking at the bookends of change, if there were no challenges or risks in the current situation and no future benefits, why would you put any effort into change? On the other end, if there was a lot of challenges and risks in a current situation and a long list of benefits in the future state, much effort could be put into the change for the personal payoff.

I would also point out that in many cases the effort to change is not as much as we make it out to be in our state of current familiarity. If diverse perspectives are leveraged to help navigate the change, the effort is much less and the future benefits much greater than expected. By looking through the windshield of opportunity instead of the rearview mirror of past comfort or familiarity, you should be better able to take appropriate action and also identify additional issues that may need to be addressed along the way, making you the hero to those who benefit from the improved change process which probably will include yourself!

Consider evaluating the challenges within your current situation and the future benefits if change is managed well. The evaluation of your current state and future rewards are parts of discovering what can or should occur and provides the motivation to make change happen. Identify "what's in it for me" and eliminate any barriers or resistance to change. This assessment can make a fundamental difference in determining the amount of effort your positive change will require.

Carefully review the diagram on the next page. If change is what you want, then this may be the key to getting that journey underway.

The Personal Formula for Change is all about Benefits, Effort, and Future Positive Results, and should be a living example of enjoying Greater Results with Less Effort.

The Personal Formula for Change
Enjoy Greater Results with Less Effort

The **B**enefits (ROI or Return on Investment) of Change
must be greater than the **E**ffort to Change
(the tool or process)
in order to yield **F**uture Positive Results.

B > E = F

An assessment of your challenge helps define the efforts needed to achieve future positive results.

Embrace the tool or process that is used to yield positive change.

When I was in college the Reserve Officers' Training Corps (ROTC) provided an opportunity for students to rappel down the side of a three-story building on campus. If you have ever rappelled, the hardest part is *starting*. You have the gloves on with your hands in front of you and behind you as you hold onto the rope at the edge of the building. Then you are asked to lean back and let the rope stretch. It is not a natural thing to do but if you have "faith in the rope," you lean back and the rope stretches, putting you at the proper position with legs against the wall. Then the descent becomes exciting and easy!

> Identify "what's in it for me." Eliminate any barriers or resistance to change. This assessment can make a fundamental difference in determining the amount of effort your positive change will require.

*****

I hope you discover that the reward of improving your future state is greater than your current threshold of challenge or the familiarity of living within your current challenges. I trust that your improvement will bring more enjoyment to your journey and build a better you. I also hope that the efforts required of you to change may not be as monumental as they first may have appeared to be, and that this truth has lowered your fear of changing and given you confidence. If true, a natural outcome would be that you are motivated to take action to improve behaviors in order to yield better outcomes for you and others.

May you apply your *heart* and *hustle* to **The Ten Bedrock Truths** that resonate with you. If you do, I am confident you will experience more enjoyment on your journey no matter what circumstances come your way.

Enjoy your journey.
Experience *Greater Results with Less Effort.*

Here's the point: when the next opportunity for change comes your way, objectively assess the current challenges and future benefits as you
identify the efforts required for change to occur.
Have "faith in the rope."
Remember: the "rope" is the tool or process that is used to start and enact the change.
Enjoy the benefits of your improvement!

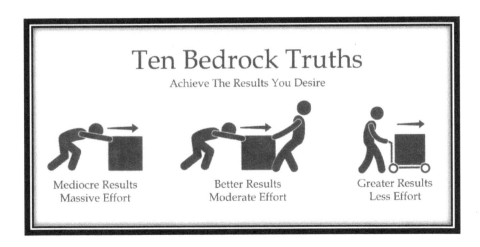

~ Graphic concept by Brett Hendrickson, 2021.

Acknowledgements

This book is the result of me responding to a request of a good friend of mine, Glen Aubrey, about sharing ten quotes or life lessons that have impacted my life. One Sunday after worship, within a week after I met with him, I sat down to the computer and typed up my responses to Glen, never thinking it would result in writing a book about **The Ten Bedrock Truths** I have lived by. Without Glen's help and guidance, this book would not have become a reality. I have shed a lot of happy tears in its writing and will be forever grateful for this experience.

To market a book like this, it is critical to have an effective website. This is not my core competency and I was thankful for the great service and guidance of Randy Beck of My Domain Tools, www.MyDomainTools.com.

I would also like to acknowledge the impact and joy my two boys have brought and continue to bring to my life. I am looking forward to seeing them continue to grow and enjoy their life journey.

I also want to acknowledge all the great role models that have demonstrated living life well and were an example to emulate. The role models started with parents, but along the way included coaches, managers, coworkers, family, and friends. These people invested in us, invited us into their homes, shared life with us, and we have laughed and cried and grown together.

*****

About the Author

Bud Hendrickson, February 17, 2021

Bud Hendrickson is passionate about enjoying life's journey. He is the youngest of seven children with six older sisters. He was raised in a one-bathroom house next to the family business where he developed his strong work ethic at an early age. Raised in a small town, Bud played three sports while in high school while also working to earn money to put gas in his car.

After being baptized just before getting married, both Bud and his wife enjoyed a spiritual growth journey together that laid a foundation upon which to build his bedrock truths.

A family man with a career in Engineering and Maintenance Leadership, Bud has worked in numerous industries. He graduated from South Dakota School of Mines and Technology with a degree in Mechanical Engineering in May of 1988.

Bud is the proud father of two sons. He is a sports enthusiast, really enjoys high school football and the Denver Broncos. His life's events are varied like everyone's, filled with the good and the bad. One of the toughest moments was enduring the loss of his high school sweetheart and wife of 28 years, Nancy, in 2015 to cancer.

With patience and purposeful actions, Bud again found a supportive life partner to enjoy life with, and one with whom he could build a better version of himself. He found this in Kristin. Kristin's life road was much different than Bud's; she was single and never married into her 50s. Their life's journeys were totally different from one another's, and they found themselves at a crossroad with God, in a married relationship, embarking on a new life journey as one.

Their next chapter included job changes for both of them. They are looking at becoming business partners. Both Bud and Kristin are optimistic about the opportunity to invest into each other's success every day. This change has not come without some in-depth research, discussion, and reflection since it is new for both of them. But in the end, they are able to make a decision considering both of their needs and being in alignment with God's will.

Most people realize that pain and pleasure are integral and often integrated parts of living. Bud chooses daily to enjoy his journey no matter what, and teaches others to do the same.

The Ten Bedrock Truths may revolutionize your understanding of how you live, and help you improve in ways you may have never dreamed possible.

*****

Products and Services

www.GreaterResultsLessEffort.com

The mission of our website is to inform and motivate individuals to make better decisions that return more enjoyment and improved results in their lives both personally and professionally. Do you want more enjoyment and more impact from the decisions in your life? Do you want a workforce or team that works for everyone's success? Apply **The Ten Bedrock Truths** to harness the potential in any person and any situation!

Contact Bud Hendrickson to schedule presentations for your group.

Detailed Topics Covered in Training and Speeches:
- o Obtaining positive results from both good and challenging situations
- o Using conflict resolution to build better relationships that benefit all involved and help to come up with better solutions in the process
- o Tapping into the awesome potential of diverse perspectives to make more informed decisions and achieve greater success

o   Learning how working hard and doing the right things bring unplanned opportunities.

o   Exercising time and money management that gives you the space to make better decisions and achieve more enjoyment

o   Becoming a better leader to inspire people to give their time and talent freely and fully

Audience:

Bud Hendrickson's message is simple and easily applied by young and old alike.

o   Corporate Leadership and Staff

o   Young Professionals

o   Colleges

o   High Schools

o   Athletic Associations

o   Church Groups

o   For-profit and Non-profit Organizations

Access **www.GreaterResultsLessEffort.com** and follow Bud Hendrickson as he demonstrates how to apply **The Ten Bedrock Truths** to the opportunities in your world. Learn how to best leverage them for your benefit and for the benefit of people around you.

Addendum:

Leadership and Teams

An Article by Bud Hendrickson for Leaders and Teams in the Workplace

Big Windshield Looking Forward and Small Mirror Looking Back

One of the **Ten Bedrock Truths** permeating my career is the need to approach life from the viewpoint of the driver's seat, with a "big windshield looking forward and a small rearview mirror looking back." This truth has gained more relevance considering the challenging year we all have endured. To effectively lead entering the summer of 2021, let's recognize key learning points from 2020 and early 2021. Looking back will help us better navigate going forward.

Studies have been conducted on the productivity of employees, and how well people have adapted to remote work, hybrid work, or working safely in person when work requires one to commute to the job. Data also exists that shows how effective some employees have been in being self-directed and autonomous in their work.

These successes should be celebrated! I recommend that all teams and individuals document the positives that have emerged from the changes in how work was accomplished in the last year with your organization, and develop plans and actions so all can be purposeful in retaining key lessons as we move forward.

Numerous studies illustrate how employees have adapted well using the new technology in working from home while maintaining the quality of content and productivity. As with all results of studies, there are other lessons to learn when data is approached from another direction. We have from 28% to 40% of the workforce who are struggling with adapting to the new ways of work.

Can your team perform at its best long term with this many team members struggling in the new work environment we've had to create? Further, is there anything new we can learn from what didn't work in the last year with the vast changes in how work was done?

Our issues essentially fall into three buckets.

1. One bucket: **those workers who have challenges with learning new technology**.

2. Another bucket: **those who lack the skills to be self-directed or autonomous**.

3. The third bucket affects many or most of our people: **missing relationships or simply not being connected to others**. Focus on relationships since history has shown **when people feel connected, they perform their best and feel their best**.

Whether an employee works remotely, cannot visit family or friends with health issues which limits the ability to be together, restrictions on travel or entertainment, and additional problems affecting our world, many feel isolated and possess a deep need for connection.

Permit me to ask: "As a leader, what are some purposeful alterations we can consider as we move forward, where life and work have dramatically changed and, in some cases, have altered permanently?" Areas of focus can and should be applied in all situations. However, they are even more important in remote/hybrid work patterns and in home-life environments in which we find ourselves currently.

Communication:

For centuries we have discussed how important communication is. Tools change, speeds at which communication is expected have increased, and the distance covered is much greater today, more than ever before. The fundamentals have not changed. In effective communication, and in moments of stress and challenge, the fundamentals are as important as they have ever been.

> **The fundamentals have not changed**.

Communication is composed of three components:

1. Words (what is actually said)
2. Tone of voice (how we say the words)
3. Body language (gestures, postures, and facial expressions that communicate non-verbally to others)

Let me inquire: "With modern technology, are we missing key communication attributes by not being in person while communicating?" "Further, with expanding use of email, virtual meetings, and remote work, are we missing key information about the health and wellbeing of our team?"

If we are not purposeful in our use of the technology and being emotionally present, we risk missing much key information. The answer: Be diligent, noticing people's gestures, facial expressions, and comments that are out of character. There may be a need to connect with them privately if you think they could benefit with some assistance or support. So, let me ask you, "Are the ground rules current for effective communication, or do they need updated and revisited by your team? Looking back over

2020, are the identified ground rules being followed?" "If not, what is the next action to create a better environment for everyone?" Awareness and small changes, with appropriate follow-up, could be the forward navigation that steers us away from future chaos and team division.

> Awareness and small changes, with appropriate follow-up, could be the forward navigation that steers us away from future chaos and team division.

Connection:

Examples exist professionally and personally where technology has been utilized to enhance communication when we cannot be "in person." We have data to show how productive most have been during the challenging times of 2020. But we don't talk much about losing connection professionally and personally.

Many work from home. Limits have been imposed on visitation of family members who reside in care facilities. We've experienced confines of seeing family and friends who live far away, or even worse, become hospitalized where visitation is strictly curtailed or prohibited altogether.

As humans we are designed to connect and be social. In everyday life, we don't see many faces because they are covered with masks. We miss facial expressions that are key elements of communication.

My encouragement: Look in your past and identify events or activities which brought connection to your team members. From your "being present" efforts to better communicate, inquire: "Have you gathered information on individuals or regarding team issues which have negative effects?"

Being proactive in identifying ways to connect your employees socially and emotionally helps ensure the health of your team on personal levels. This allows them to interact with individuals at work at their highest levels of engagement.

Care:

We all know how much better we feel when we know someone cares about us, as people. When we are happier and feel safe, we become more resilient, energetic, and innovative. We need these qualities, not only in ourselves, but in everyone with whom we interact.

To help with this connection, let's allow for some open time for people to share about themselves regarding something *not* related to work. Schedule an event to donate money and/or time to a worthy cause valued by the team members. Adopt attitudes of service to others.

Community:

There are great needs in all of our communities today! What better way to connect with others than to *work together for a common good*?

Focus. Keep looking through the windshield during these challenging times. Our shared experiences last year could provide key information to help you and others navigate better as we all move forward to better times.

Create a Catalyst for Others Around You!

The efforts you make personally to better communicate, connect, care, and be a more vibrant part of community *will* build a better you. Building a better you is key. These efforts could <u>form the catalyst for others around you to do the</u> <u>same</u>.

*****

www.GreaterResultsLessEffort.com

*****

CPSIA information can be obtained
at www.ICGtesting.com
Printed in the USA
BVHW031517260421
605863BV00007B/1368

9 780985 597955